The Church Fathers are
of availability but for lack
there is simply too great a
to warrant the effort to find a way across. As a result, evangelicals
remain separated from many of their earlier brothers and sisters
that could serve as helpful and encouraging guides along the
Way of Truth. This is why I am thankful for Marvin Jones and
this new work, *Basil of Caesarea*. Jones's introduction to the life
and thought of this Church Father serves well as the book to
grab to review forgotten facts or learn of Basil for the first time.
I am glad to have it on my shelf.

Jason G. Duesing
Assistant Professor of Historical Theology,
Southwestern Baptist Theological Seminary, Fort Worth, Texas

Marvin Jones' lucid account of Basil introduces us not just to the
subtlety and real acuity of Basil's thought but to a man of great
warmth and affection. Theologically, Christians today continue
to owe a huge debt to Basil's work and this book explains why.
We also meet a follower of Christ whose commitment to the right
honour and praise of our triune God was costly at a personal
level and who therefore challenges us as well as instructs us.

Michael Ovey
Principal, Oak Hill Theological College, London

Marvin Jones introduces Basil of Caesarea to a new generation
of readers in a clear representation of Basil's theology. Basil's
bishopric was pivotal in the development of doctrine, particularly that of the Spirit, and Jones traces his contributions to
the benefit of the reader, who encounters Basil as a lover of the
Triune God and His church.

Steven A. McKinion
Associate Professor of Theology and Patristic Studies,
Southeastern Baptist Theological Seminary, Wake Forest, North Carolina

If Basil of Caesarea had written but one book, his *On the Holy Spirit* – the first book specifically devoted to the person of the Spirit of God – a book like this one by Dr. Jones would be needed to explicate the theology of Basil's tome. Basil's theological vision played a vital role in shaping the pneumatology of the creed issued at the Council of Constantinople and has thus had enormous influence in the history of the Church. But Basil's ministry was also of vital importance in reforming monasticism and defending a full-blooded Trinitarianism in the days after the death of the Trinity's great champion Athanasius. In addition to all of this, we know more about Basil than any other Christian of the ancient church apart from Augustine of Hippo, due to a marvelous collection of some 350 letters. We have then all of the makings of an important story that Evangelicals need to hear and ponder. And Dr. Jones has done us Evangelicals a great favor in writing this lucid account of Basil's life and theology. A good reminder that the Fathers are an important part of the family tree of those people who call themselves Evangelical.

Michael A.G. Haykin
Professor of Church History & Biblical Spirituality,
& Director of The Andrew Fuller Center for Baptist Studies,
The Southern Baptist Theological Seminary, Louisville, Kentucky

EARLY CHURCH FATHERS

BASIL OF CAESAREA

His Life and Impact

Marvin Jones

Series editor:
Michael A. G. Haykin

Marvin Jones is Chair of the Christian Studies Department and Assistant Professor of Church History and Theology at Louisiana College in Pineville, Louisiana. He holds degrees from Southeastern Baptist Theological Seminary, Dallas Theological Seminary and the University of South Africa.

paperback ISBN 978-1-78191-302-4
epub ISBN 978-1-78191-371-0
Mobi ISBN 978-1-78191-372-7

First published in 2014
by
Christian Focus Publications Ltd,
Geanies House, Fearn, Ross-shire
IV20 1TW, Scotland
www.christianfocus.com

A CIP catalogue record for this book is available from the British Library.

Cover artwork illustrator: Hélène Grondines
Cover designer: Daniel van Straaten

Printed by Bell and Bain, Glasgow

CONTENTS

DEDICATION

This book is dedicated to three special people who have supported not only the endeavor but the author.

To

my wife, Stacy

God's blessing to me and partner in ministry. May the Lord keep you safe in body and lovable in spirit.

To

Marshall, my son

A young man who loves God's outdoors, a good workout, and displays a quiet but deep faith. May God continue to bless your life with profound simplicity of heart.

To

McKenzie, my daughter

I have no doubt that someday you will conquer your part of the world. Until then your gift of laughter is my blessing. May the Lord continue to allow you to have a sweet, yet aggressive disposition.

SERIES PREFACE

On reading the Church Fathers

By common definition, the Church Fathers are those early
Christian authors who wrote between the close of the first
century, right after the death of the last of the apostles, namely
the apostle John, and the middle of the eighth century. In other
words, those figures who were active in the life of the church
between Ignatius of Antioch and Clement of Rome, who
penned writings at the very beginning of the second century,
and the Venerable Bede and John of Damascus, who stood at
the close of antiquity and the onset of the Middle Ages. Far
too many Evangelicals in the modern day know next to nothing
about these figures. I will never forget being asked to give a mini-
history conference at a church in southern Ontario. I suggested
three talks on three figures from Latin-speaking North Africa:
Perpetua, Cyprian, and Augustine. The leadership of the church
came back to me seeking a different set of names, since they
had never heard of the first two figures, and while they had
heard of the third name, the famous bishop of Hippo Regius,
they really knew nothing about him. I gave them another list of

post-Reformation figures for the mini-conference, but privately thought that not knowing anything about these figures was possibly a very good reason to have a conference on them! I suspect that such ignorance is quite widespread among those who call themselves Evangelicals – hence the importance of this small series of studies on a select number of Church Fathers, to educate and inform God's people about their forebears in the faith.

Past appreciation for the Fathers

How different is the modern situation from the past, when many of our Evangelical and Reformed forebears knew and treasured the writings of the ancient church. The French Reformer John Calvin, for example, was ever a keen student of the Church Fathers. He did not always agree with them, even when it came to one of his favorite authors, namely, Augustine. But he was deeply aware of the value of knowing their thought and drawing upon the riches of their written works for elucidating the Christian faith in his own day. And in the seventeenth century, the Puritan theologian John Owen, rightly called the 'Calvin of England' by some of his contemporaries, was not slow to turn to the experience of the one he called 'holy Austin,' namely Augustine, to provide him with a pattern of God the Holy Spirit's work in conversion.

Yet again, when the Particular Baptist John Gill was faced with the anti-Trinitarianism of the Deist movement in the early eighteenth century, and other Protestant bodies – for instance, the English Presbyterians, the General Baptists, and large tracts of Anglicanism – were unable to retain a firm grasp on this utterly vital biblical doctrine, Gill turned to the Fathers to help him elucidate the biblical teaching regarding the blessed Trinity. Gill's example in this regard influenced other Baptists such as John Sutcliff, pastor of the Baptist cause in Olney, where John Newton also ministered. Sutcliff was so impressed by the *Letter* to *Diognetus*, which he wrongly supposed to have been written by Justin Martyr, that he translated it for *The Biblical Magazine*, a Calvinistic publication with a small circulation. He sent it to the editor of this periodical with the commendation that this second-century work is 'one of the most valuable pieces of ecclesiastical antiquity.'

One final caveat

One final word about the Fathers recommended in this small series of essays. The Fathers are not Scripture. They are senior conversation partners about Scripture and its meaning. We listen to them respectfully, but are not afraid to disagree when they err. As the Reformers rightly argued, the writings of the Fathers must be subject to Scripture. John Jewel, the Anglican apologist, put it well when he stated in 1562:

> But what say we of the fathers, Augustine, Ambrose, Jerome, Cyprian, etc.? What shall we think of them, or what account may we make of them? They be interpreters of the word of God. They were learned men, and learned fathers; the instruments of the mercy of God, and vessels full of grace. We despise them not, we read them, we reverence them, and give thanks unto God for them. They were witnesses unto the truth, they were worthy pillars and ornaments in the church of God. Yet may they not be compared with the word of God. We may not build upon them: we may not make them the foundation and warrant of our conscience: we may not put our trust in them. Our trust is in the name of the Lord.

Michael A. G. Haykin
The Southern Baptist Theological Seminary
Louisville, Kentucky.

ACKNOWLEDGMENTS

This book would not be possible without the help and encouragement of several people. The first that deserves recognition is Dr. Michael Haykin. He and I met at an Andrew Fuller conference on the campus of Southern Baptist Theological Seminary in 2008. We had dinner and engaged in casual conversation. During the course of the evening, he learned that I had written my dissertation on Athanasius. Within the next three weeks, he issued a generous offer to write this current volume on Basil. Michael has been an encourager, polite critic, source of information, and a true blessing in ways that I cannot possibly recount. My prayerful desire is that our friendship continues to grow in the rich fellowship of Christ.

While being surprised by the blessings of God in Louisville, the Lord prepared the way for me to start another Ph.D. program in Fort Worth, Texas. The challenge of such an endeavor has its own unique hurdles. However, in addition to the normal inherent difficulties, the complication of this new program was that I had to fly from Atlanta to Dallas on a weekly basis. I lived in Chattanooga, commuted to Atlanta, and boarded a plane to

Dallas in order to work on the Ph.D. at Southwestern Baptist Theological Seminary.

The commute to Dallas Fort Worth was made easy and pleasurable because of the sacrifice of my family in Dallas. My mother, who provided a place to stay, my sisters (and their husbands), who provided shuttle services and good company, were and are a blessing, then and now. While I attended seminars and worked on this project, they provided love, friendship, food, laughter, and a second home. This work would have suffered if not for Mom (Judy Jones), Krista and Roy, Sheila and Javier, and Tawanna and Kevin. I must mention Leslie, my niece, and Ryan, my nephew, for providing comic relief, street racing opportunities, and just good fun for their uncle. My other nephew, Christian, and my other nieces, Whitney and Courtney, were at college and did contact me on occasion. They were delightful and encouraging. Thank you for helping the prodigal son, brother, and uncle.

While commuting to Dallas Fort Worth on a weekly basis, I still maintained a teaching position at Luther Rice University (L.R.U.). Dr. James Flanagan, President of Luther Rice University, encouraged me to work on that program, and this book, all the while bending the rules so that I could accomplish both goals. He is a blessing to all who know him. Another person of constant encouragement at L.R.U. is Ms. Sherri Humphrey. She is the faculty secretary and quite honestly I have concluded that the ship would not sail nearly as efficiently without her ministry. She edited this manuscript, made grammatical suggestions, and helped me complete this overwhelming task. A heartfelt 'thank you' to Ms. Humphrey, Dr. Flanagan, and the faculty at L.R.U. is long overdue. So, 'Thank you.' Maybe someday I can return the blessing.

The effable and affable Dr. Paige Patterson has been, and I am certain will continue to be, an encourager, friend, tough critic, merciful judge, and all-around role model. I have known the man for twenty-five years and during that time he has chided and encouraged me always with the love of Christ. I have witnessed the man do the same for countless others. Thank you for writing the foreword and thank you for loving a young preacher 'way back when' and an older one now.

On a personal note, my immediate family has watched in anticipation, waited for the final product, encouraged me to write, and demanded at times that I take a break, and yet keep focused upon the book. Their consistent promptings to write and their sporadic times of forcing me to get away from the work have contributed much to this book. Also, thank you to my prayer warrior and mother-in-law, Mrs. Arlene Allen.

Finally, I wish to thank the Lord Jesus Christ for calling me to the ministry, equipping me educationally, and allowing me to engage in the life of a preacher. In the process of being a pastor, the Lord directed me to study the Church Fathers. That fateful day came as a result of a need in the pastoral ministry. It was almost as if the Lord was saying to me, 'There have been many others who have walked the pathway of faith. Learn from them.' As I started re-reading the New Testament with freshness, I encountered the passion of souls that motivated Paul and saw it in the life of Athanasius, who had the same passion for the truth. The quest for truth was and hopefully always will be soteriological. That passion and legacy was 'passed on' to Basil and hopefully it can be reclaimed today. Thank you, Lord.

Marvin Jones
Ringgold, Georgia
3 February 2013

FOREWORD

Most people view various periods of antiquity through the rose-colored lens of distance and therefore form a perspective of history that often at best is a caricature of that era. The patristic era is no exception. In fact, so crucial were the issues, particularly the Christological debates, that the various creeds adopted by the church through the years take on the aura of a halo. The result is that figures of history such as Basil, Augustine, Chrysostom, and others assume a larger-than-life posture, and the average churchman forgets or never realizes that these men were merely men. They were the pawns of the cultures of their time, victims and sometimes victors of the politics of the populace, and players in the ecclesiastical confrontations of ideas that shaped the period. They had convictions, but they also had passions that sometimes shaped or distorted their own perspectives. Caught in the webs of intrigue and speculation, 'ecclesiastical politics' vied with purer motives and genuine pastoral concerns for hegemony in the mind and heart. In short, they differed precious little from their counterparts in the present era.

Sensing the need to illumine the life and convictions of one of the most important fathers, Marvin Jones provides a basic introduction to the colorful story of Basil of Caesarea and documents the various controversies in which Basil found himself involved. Painting a vivid picture of the controversies of the fourth century, Jones makes the era come to life for the reader. Introducing the reader to the biographical facts of Basil's life, Jones evaluates the impact of monasticism on the life of the saint. The reader has the opportunity to know Basil personally.

Then, utilizing three of the major terms of the Christological debate, Jones walks through the nuances of the changing face of Basil's own views. Jones describes the first phase as the *homoiousian* phase, the second as the *homoousian* phase, and the third as the *hypostasis* phase. Readers are assisted by Jones in comprehending the essence of the arguments surrounding these terms and the development of Basil's own perspective.

Marvin Jones also is aware of the considerable contributions of Basil to the doctrine of pneumatology. These he delineates with consummate skill. Focusing on the years of Basil's sojourn in the desert, the author examines, in addition, the impact of those who sought God in the solitude of the wilderness. Jones finds at numerous points in Basil's thinking insights for modern Evangelical Christianity. Finally, he discusses Basil's influence in the modern era.

A major work on Basil is a welcome addition to the library of anyone with a curiosity about church history, but this volume is also abounding with pastoral wisdom and with the discussion of theological themes important to any era and not to be ignored. Moreover, this is an insightful study in human nature and how men of God respond to the shifting sands of the theological and ecclesiastical landscape. May God grant that this book be read as it was written – a critical but sympathetic assessment of a remarkable pilgrim on life's journey.

Paige Patterson, President
Southwestern Baptist Theological Seminary
Fort Worth, Texas

1

BASIL'S LIFE: AN OVERVIEW

Basil the confident man of God

The year was A.D. 372 and the political climate of the region
of Cappadocia was such that a confrontation was imminent.
Valens had struck terror in the hearts of Nicene Orthodox pastors. He persecuted them, banished them, and even martyred
some of them. In 372, his target was Caesarea. Only one person
stood in his way, a man of remarkable integrity, profound ministry accomplishments, and a man who, by his strong confidence
in God, could defy the Emperor – Basil of Caesarea.

The Prefect, Modestus, charged by the Emperor Valens,
demanded that Basil should communicate and work with Arian
bishops. The modern person may find it difficult to understand
the dynamics of the problem. However, the issue of Arianism (to be
discussed later) was at the forefront of a political and ecclesiastical
agenda. Basil, summoned to appear before Modestus, answered
for his actions of resisting the Emperor. The Prefect asked Basil to
explain how he could 'dare, as no other dares, to resist and oppose
so great a potentate?'[1] Basil inquired about the accusation, to

---

1. Gregory of Nazianzen, *The Panegyric on St. Basil*, translated by Charles Gordon
   Browne and James Edward Swallow in *Saint Gregory of Nazianzen*, eds. Philip Schaff
   and Henry Wace, *Nicene and Post-Nicene Christianity* (NPNF), vol. 7 (Peabody, MA:
   Hendrickson Publishers, 2006), p. 411.

which Modestus replied that he had 'refused to respect the religion of your sovereign, when all others have yielded and submitted themselves.'[2] In a play on words that seemed to be designed to demonstrate the difference between God and an emperor, Basil stated, 'Because this is not the will of my real Sovereign nor can I, who am the creature of God, and bidden myself to be God, submit to worship any creature.'[3]

As the conversation continued, Modestus grew impatient and angry with Basil. In harsh words, Modestus screamed, 'What? Have you no fear of my authority?' 'Fear of what? (Basil's reply)'[4] There is no doubt that Modestus was trying to intimidate a bishop who simply could not be intimidated. The Prefect continued his rants, 'Of what? Of any one of the resources of my power' (Modestus' answer to Basil's question).[5] Here is where Basil inquires of the power of the Prefect. What power and what resources does the Prefect Modestus have that can persuade Basil to cooperate with the Emperor's demands? Modestus answered with a scare tactic, 'Confiscation, banishment, torture, death.'[6]

Basil realized that his calling was of God so that his perspective on ministry, life, and certainly his position before a hostile government, was directed by the providence of the Lord. He replied to Modestus, 'Have you no other threat? For none of these can reach me.' To which the astonished Modestus replied, 'How indeed is that?' Basil's answer reveals not only the trust he has in God but the depth of commitment to his calling to serve God. He stated:

> Because a man who has nothing, is beyond the reach of confiscation; unless you demand my tattered rags, and the few books, which are my only possessions. Banishment is impossible for me,

---

2. Gregory of Nazianzen, *The Panegyric on St. Basil*, p. 411.

3. Ibid.

4. Ibid.

5. Ibid.

6. Ibid.

who am confined by no limit of place, counting my own neither the land where I now dwell, nor all of that into which I may be hurled; or, rather, counting it all God's whose guest and dependent I am. As for tortures, what hold can they have upon one whose body has ceased to be? Unless you mean the first stroke, for this alone is in your power. Death is my benefactor, for it will send me the sooner to God, for Whom I live, and exist, and have all but died, and to Whom I have long been hastening.[7]

Modestus did not know what or how to reply. All he could say was simply that no man had ever spoken to him in such a way. Basil's reply has become a classic statement in the annals of Christianity. Basil replied, 'Perhaps you have never met with a Bishop, or in his defense of such interest he would have used precisely the same language.'[8] One cannot help but wonder if Basil was describing that a true bishop would make a stand with such confidence as opposed to the Arian bishops who capitulated to the imperial decrees and demands of a godless emperor.

Such was the political climate of the latter fourth century. What had transpired in the Empire is that God prepared a man to confront the political and ecclesiastical culture of the era—an era which started at a bridge!

Fourth-century Rome

Constantine, the Roman Emperor, heavily influenced the political environment during the first third of the fourth century. He played a vital role in legitimatizing the Christian faith.[9] In the infamous battle of the Milvian Bridge, which took place in October of 312, he solidified his reign. An imperial power struggle had developed in the Empire between Constantine and Maxentius. Constantine had decided to attack Maxentius at Rome. He

---

7.   Gregory of Nazianzen, *The Panegyric on St. Basil*, p. 411.

8.   Ibid.

9.   Harold O. J. Brown, *Heresies* (Garden City, NY: Doubleday & Co, 1984), p. 108.

advanced toward the city unaware that his enemy was superior militarily and that they had occupied the Milvian Bridge. In desperation, Constantine turned to the Christian God for help. Bruce Shelley wrote, 'In a dream, he saw a cross in the sky and the words, "In this sign conquer." When on 28 October 312 he achieved his brilliant victory over the troops of Maxentius, Constantine looked upon his success as proof of the power of Christ and the superiority of the Christian religion.'[10]

Constantine: Known as Constantine the Great, he conquered his rival Maxentius at the Milvian Bridge to become co-ruler of the Roman Empire in A.D. 312. In a personal dream, his victory was secure only if he fought under the sign of the cross. He attributed his victory to the Christian God; subsequently, in 313, along with co-ruler Licinius, he issued the Edict of Milan allowing the toleration of Christianity. This action gave the Christian church much freedom, but it also forged the union between church and state. The end result was that Constantine was known to settle ecclesiastical matters as ruler of the Roman Empire. His most famous intervention is known as the Council of Nicea, called in 325. This council dealt with the problem of Arius and Arianism.

As a result of the battle of the Milvian Bridge, the famous 'Edict of Milan' was mandated into law. This edict gave religious toleration, even freedom, to all religions of that day. At the time, the Roman Empire had only two rulers: (1) Constantine

---

10. Bruce Shelley, *Church History in Plain Language* (Dallas, TX: Word Publishing, 1982), p. 108. At the death of Galerius, who was a contemporary of Constantine's father, Constantius Chlorus, a civil war broke out over who would control the Roman Empire. This specific battle, in the life of Constantine, had direct ramifications for the Council of Nicea. If Constantine had lost the battle, it is safe to assume that the Nicene Council might never have convened. Galerius, unlike Constantius Chlorus, continued the Diocletian persecution and passed this legacy to Maxentius. While not desiring to imply the proverbial 'good versus evil' epic, this writer is convinced that the providence of God clearly is evident in the history that proceeds from these events.

(favoring the Christians while tolerating the pagans) who ruled in the west and (2) Licinius (favoring the pagans and tolerating the Christians) who ruled in the east.

Constantine's leadership proved beneficial for the advancement of the church as Christians enjoyed more freedom than at any point in history. Constantine exempted the clergy from military duty, abolished laws that were offensive to Christians, emancipated Christian slaves, and enjoined Sunday as a day of worship.

The Roman Empire politically was secure under the leadership of Constantine. Both east and west enjoyed the tranquility of a peaceful life as Constantine ruled a unified Roman Empire. The unity of the Empire was predicated on two fronts: (1) political and military solidarity was achieved as there was no inward or outward threat to the Empire and (2) Christianity now was accepted openly without the fear of government or private persecution. Thus, in the mind of Constantine, the religion of the people could maintain the moral climate of good citizenship. Seemingly, peace and comfort was in place for Constantine, the Roman Empire, and the Christian Church.

Fourth-century ecclesiological conflict

Harold O. J. Brown wrote, 'No sooner had Constantine, the first Christian Emperor, gained complete control of the Empire than he found the church – which he had hoped would help him reunite his vast domain – riven by bitter conflict.'[11] The church was nearing an entrance into a period of intense theological debate. Prior to the fourth century, most of the challenges to the church were external, coming from individuals or groups outside of Christianity. The theological debate of the early fourth century was internal and found its appeal and support from the clergy within Christianity.

---

11. Brown, *Heresies*, pp. 107-8.

Arianism

The debate during this period centred upon the views of Arius. Due to the fact that Arius was the presbyter of the Baucalis Church in Alexandria, William Rusch noted, 'The outset of the controversy, probably in about the year 319, was caused by Arius' preaching.'[12] The content of his sermons became the foundation for the heresy known as Arianism.[13]

> **Arius:** Arius was a student at the well known Antiochian School as a pupil of Lucian. Following his tenure at Antioch, he became bishop of Baucalis at Alexandria, Egypt, and began to teach his deviant Christology. Arius concluded that there 'was a time when the Son was not,' which means that Arius denied the eternal existence of the second person of the Trinity. He denied the Son existed eternally with the Father. He taught that the Father created the Son, in time, and that the Son had a different nature than the Father. Thus, Arius taught that the Son was a creature who was created at the highest order of the Father but nonetheless a creature. This protected the monarchy of the Father at the expense of the eternality of the Son. This teaching soon became known as Arianism.

Arius adhered to a deviant position concerning the nature of Jesus Christ within the Godhead. Louis Berkhof described Arius' views of Christ when he wrote, 'His dominant idea was the monotheistic principle of the Monarchians, that there is only one unbegotten God, one unoriginated Being, without any beginning existence.'[14] Arius attempted to preserve the monotheism of God without considering the possibility of the Son being the same substance as God.

---

12. William G. Rusch, *The Trinitarian Controversy* (Philadelphia, PA: Fortress Press, 1980), p. 17.

13. The Arian Controversy was named after the proclamation of Arius' theological content of his sermons. Since he was known as the central figure in the controversy, the heresy which he expounded was named after him. However, history has recorded that Arius followed the teachings of Lucian, who was influenced by Paul of Samosata. Thus, Arius does not seem to be the originator of his views but he certainly did popularize them.

14. Louis Berkhof, *The History of Christian Doctrines* (Grand Rapids, MI: Baker Book House Publishing Co, 1996), p. 84.

The Arian Doctrine

Some may find it difficult to argue that Arius was insincere in his task to preserve the monotheism of God the Father while trying to examine the relationship of the Logos-Christ to the Father. The only conclusion for Arius was to emphasize the difference between the essence of the Father and of the Son. Arius forced this difference to its most logical conclusion: the Son was a created being. In a letter to Alexander, Arius wrote the following:

> God being the cause of all is without beginning, most alone; but the Son, begotten by the Father, created and founded before the ages, was not before He was begotten. Rather, the Son begotten timelessly, alone was caused to subsist by the Father. For He is not everlasting or co-everlasting or unbegotten with the Father. Nor does He have being with the Father, as certain individuals mention things relatively and bring into the discussion two unbegotten causes.[15]

The Arian doctrine can be summarized in four main points. First, the Son is a creature. Second, the Son had a beginning. Third, the Son does not have direct knowledge of God the Father. Fourth, the Son is liable to sin. Arius succeeded in preserving the monotheism of God the Father. However, he forfeited the deity of the second person of the Trinity, Jesus Christ. Instead, Arius introduced a half-god, half-man, so that, through Arius' preaching, the Christian church was worshiping a demigod.

The well-known dictum that describes the Arian position regarding the Son is, 'There was a time when he was not.'[16] The occasion for the infamous phrase was a public worship service at which the Bishop of Alexandria, Alexander, was preaching on the subject of the Trinity. Arius may have assumed that Alexander was introducing

15. Arius. *Letter to Alexander.* Edited and Translated by William G Rusch. In *The Trinitarian Controversy.* (Philadelphia, PA: Fortress Press, 1980), pp. 31-2.

16. J. N. D. Kelly, *Early Christian Doctrines* (San Francisco, CA: Harper Collins Publishing, 1978), p. 228.

the heretical doctrine of Sabellianism.[17] In contradiction to the Trinitarian message of Alexander, Arius uttered the famous phrase noted above. Arius even created jingles using the content of his theology so that the common person could sing them while he worked.

The actions of Arius infuriated the Bishop. Alexander, a brilliant orator, tried to overcome Arius through discussion and debate. The common ground for these men was the belief that the Logos existed prior to the incarnation. The real issue of the controversy was the relationship between the Father and Son. Arius viewed Jesus simply as a human being devoid of divine status, though coming to possess the Logos as a human. However, the Logos was not co-eternal with the Father but a creation of the Father. Thus, the Logos is separate from the Father's nature and he was given to the person of Jesus Christ.

Alexander accused Arius of worshiping something other than God. Appealing to both Scripture and tradition, Alexander argued that since the inception of Christianity, the church worshiped Jesus as God. If Jesus were less than God, Christians would be guilty of worshiping a created being. The debate was futile. As Bishop of Alexandria, Alexander had the responsibility of protecting not only the people of his own parish, but other parishes as well. In an effort to stop the spread of these aberrant teachings throughout the churches, Alexander announced a ban on Arius and his teachings.

The problem with Alexander's approach is that he underestimated the influence of Arius, who was older and, therefore, better connected politically throughout the region. Arius acquired support from Eusebius, Bishop of Nicomedia. Eusebius, in turn, wrote a letter of support for Arius stating, 'We have never heard

17. Sabellianism is a modalistic form of Monarchianism and is so named from Sabellius, of whom, however, very little is known. He was perhaps like his fellow Monarchians, Noetus and Praxeas, an early third-century theologian of Roman origin. Monarchianism propagated the concept that the differences in the Godhead were only a mere succession of existences or modes of operation of the one God. In other words, God was Father, then Son, then Holy Spirit. This denies the Trinity and places an emphasis on God transitioning to differing modes of being. See *The Oxford Dictionary of the Christian Church*, 3rd ed., under 'Sabellianism.'

that there are two unbegotten beings, nor that one has been divided into two ... yet we affirm that the unbegotten is one, and one also that which exists in truth by Him, yet was not made out of His substance.'[18] This letter prompted Alexander to send letters to all the bishops of the eastern portion of Constantine's Empire. Later, he excommunicated Arius at a synod in 321.

Constantine convenes the Council of Nicea

Emperor Constantine knew that the dispute could cause a deep rift within the Empire.[19] He could not achieve private reconciliation; therefore, according to Williston Walker, he 'decided to call a universal council of the church to settle the dispute. The synodal letter from Antioch makes mention of the synod to be held in Ancyra. But the site was transferred to Nicea before the beginning of the council.'[20]

Council of Nicea, A.D. 325: This is the first ecumenical council of the Christian church outside of the New Testament. The Emperor, Constantine, called the council to deal with the problem of Arianism in the church. The vast majority of bishops and presbyters were neutral on the issue. The Arians represented a small minority, along with Athanasius and Alexander who also represented an equally small party. The Arians, thinking victory was secure, presented their views in radical form, thus alienating the vast uncommitted majority. The Arians stated that Christ did not exist eternally with the Father and was subsequently created by the Father's will. Most of

18. Eusebius, *Letter to Paulinus, Bishop of Tyre*, translated by Blomfield Jackson in *The Ecclesiastical History, Dialogues, and Letters of Theodoret*, ed. Philip Schaff and Henry Wace, NPNF, 2nd Series, vol. 3 (Peabody, MA: Hendrickson Publishers, 1994), p. 42.

19. Constantine was so enamored with having unity among the bishops (and the Empire) that he pledged his word that the bishops and their attendants would be provided transportation at public expense. He also assured them that their necessities would be supplied.

20. Williston Walker, *A History of the Christian Church* (New York, NY: Charles Scribner's Sons Publishing, 1985), p. 133.

the majority did not have theological acumen, but knew that the details presented by the Arians were not biblical. They supported the position of Athanasius and Alexander, and adopted the Nicene Creed, which contained four anathemas: 'But those who say: "There was a time when he was not"; and "He was not before he was made"; and "He was made out of nothing," or "He is of another substance" or "essence," or "The Son of God is created," or "changeable", or "alterable"—they are condemned by the holy catholic and apostolic Church.' The positive aspect of the Nicene Creed is that it affirms Christ as God and the Holy Spirit as God. Thus the Nicene Creed is Trinitarian. The negative side is that it did not develop the Trinitarian theology in a significant manner as to anticipate the impending crisis of pneumatology in the latter half of the fourth century.

The council convened in late spring 325, with 318 bishops and presbyters in attendance. Also attending the council was a young deacon named Athanasius. He was the assistant to Alexander and wrote two classic volumes on the doctrine of theology proper: *The Incarnation* and *Against the Heathen*.

The 318 bishops seemed to represent three distinct groups at Nicea. First, there were the Arians represented by and sympathetic to Arius. Second, the Alexandrians who were represented by Athanasius. Third, the majority of the council were those who were unaligned with either group. This majority was well represented by the prestigious Eusebius of Caesarea (Eusebians for the sake of clarity). The Eusebians lacked the theological acumen of the Arians or Alexandrians.

Athanasius: He is known as the Champion of Nicea. Athanasius was mentored by Alexander of Alexandria, the personal rival of Arius. At the council of Nicea, Alexander chose Athanasius to accompany him to the council and present the position that Jesus Christ is the eternal Son of God and is God. One of his most famous works is *On The Incarnation,* which depicts the necessity of the Incarnation set in a systematic fashion. His work, *Contra Arianos*, can be justly called his magnum opus. This work deals with the logical and biblical absurdities of the Arian position. In this work, he denounces the Arian position as anti-Christian and states that it was an 'invention' unknown by the apostles.

The basic differences between the three parties can be demonstrated by their adherence to various theological positions. The Arians were convinced that the Son was a creation of God the Father and thus a *different* substance (*heteroousia*). The Alexandrians, however, believed that the Son was equal to and of the *same* substance as the Father (*homoousia*). Seemingly, the majority arrived with Arian sympathies, opposing 'the doctrine that the Son is of the same substance (*homoousios*) with the Father.'[21]

heteroousios: This word states that the Father and Son do not have a substance that is the same or even like one another. They are totally different in their natures and beings.

Eusebius of Caesarea conceded to the arguments with one caveat to the Alexandrians: the Eusebians did not accept that the Son was the *same* substance as the Father. They continued to adhere to the Son as being a *similar* substance (*homoiousios*) to the Father, an issue that would arise later in the fourth century and one with which Basil would contend.

homoousios: The basic definition is 'same substance.' The word won the day at the Council of Nicea. The definition was applied to the Son as He was/is the same substance (*homoousios*) with the Father. This word indicated that same substance was the standard definition to be applied with regard to the Trinity.

The council opened with an appeal to the bishops and presbyters for unity. The desire was to have an easy, but decisive, resolution for the church. Nonetheless, the Arians stated their convictions in the most radical terms. Brown stated, 'The Arians,

---

21. Berkhof, *The History of Christian Doctrines*, p. 86.

confident that victory would be theirs, made the great mistake of beginning the council by presenting their own statement of faith, a straightforward document drawn up by Eusebius of Nicomedia.[22] This document emphatically denied the deity of Jesus Christ. The majority, not understanding the issue at stake, did recognize the error of the Arian document. The Arian creed was voted down overwhelmingly. When the defeat became inevitable, Arius appealed to his friend Eusebius of Caesarea to write a new confession.

homoiousios: Arius presented this word as an attempt to compromise at the Council of Nicea. This word means of 'like or similar substance,' which allows a degree of separation of substance between the Father and Son. Thus, according to this word, the Father and Son do not have the same substance but something that is very similar to one another. The word, *homoiousios*, denies the ontological unity of the Father and Son.

Eusebius proposed an ancient Palestinian Confession that was similar to the Nicene Creed but avoided the term *homoousia*. According to Schaff, 'The Emperor had already seen and approved this confession, and even the Arian minority were ready to accept it.'[23] Everyone present except Alexander and Athanasius agreed to the confession. The two men believed that signing the document would compromise their conception of orthodoxy. Constantine, who sought peace within the church, realized that any chance of unity was unlikely. Therefore, in order to ratify this confession or creed, the word *homoousia* was added, an addition that affected the meaning of the document significantly.

Rumors indicated that the Bishop of Cordova, Hosius, suggested to the Emperor that the term *homoousia* be added to

22. Brown, *Heresies*, p. 117.
23. Schaff, *A History of the Christian Church*, p. 628.

placate the Alexandrian party.[24] Although Constantine listened to the suggestion of Hosius, he 'finally threw the weight of his authority into the balance and thus secured the victory for the party of Athanasius.'[25] Thus, the official orthodox creed ensured that the Son was of the same substance (*homoousia*) as the Father.

The aftermath of Nicea

Although the council established the Nicene Creed as the official orthodox position, they did not settle the Arian controversy. In fact, according to Berkhof, it was 'only the beginning of it.'[26] Part of the reason for the predicament was the Emperor himself. Constantine's desire for peace came at the expense of alienating the council members who signed the Nicene Creed but never seemed to take ownership of it. However, Arius refused to sign the creed. Although his teaching gained momentum, his refusal to sign the creed deemed it necessary for Constantine to banish him.

Arius' followers, joined with Eusebius of Caesarea, enlarged the third party and made it easier to build momentum for their position. This new middle party quickly became known as the semi-Arians. Their theological position emerged in various ways throughout the Empire.[27] The debate between the Arian party and the Athanasian party continued for the next fifty years, culminating in the Council of Constantinople in 381, in which Basil played a major role.

---

24. Most historians assert that Hosius probably influenced Constantine to utilize and employ this term. However, there is no direct evidence to make the case. In fact, Hans Lietzmann, *From Constantine to Julian* (London: Letterworth Press, 1950) suggested that Constantine deliberately chose this word because it was used in the common vernacular of the day.

25. Berkhof, *The History of Christian Doctrines*, p. 87.

26. Ibid.

27. The difference between the Arian and semi-Arian can be seen in their respective terms to describe the relationship between the Father and the Son. The Arians embraced the term *heteroousias*, which is defined as a *different* substance than the Father. Whereas, the semi-Arians preferred the term *homoiousios*, which is defined as a *like* substance of the Father. See Louis Berkhof's, *The History of Christian Doctrines*, for more detail.

Fourth-century ecclesiological conflict—phase two

During the late 350s to early 360s, the church was entering the second phase of the Arian Controversy.[28] The problem of the Arian heresy did not disappear with the conclusion of the Nicene Council.[29] The Nicene Council established the foundation of Trinitarian orthodoxy. However, it did not handle the Christological issues that arose from the proceedings, the foremost of which was how the two natures of Christ relate to one another.

Again, the challenge to Christology originated in the Arian position of the Logos. The denial of the divinity of the Logos seemed to lead the orthodox party to question both the union of the two natures and their being separate and distinct from each other.

The Council of Nicea (325) established the orthodoxy of the Son but did not address the issue of the Holy Spirit directly. In other words, one could question if the Holy Spirit is also God in the same manner as the Son. This became the theological question that took centre stage during the middle of the fourth century.

By 361, Julian ascended the throne, allowing for the possibility that the Nicene Council's orthodoxy could be challenged. The reason for this is that Julian (who has been termed 'the Apostate') wanted to return to pagan worship in the secular world. The Christian world could not give a strong rebuttal to Julian because of the inner turmoil resulting from moderate Arianism. Some of the failure for a clear orthodox position lies with inadequate terminology. The vocabulary of Nicea left numerous unresolved

---

28. For background information to the Arian Controversy, see John Behr's, *The Nicene Faith*, 2 volumes (Crestwood, NY: St. Vladimir's Seminary Press, 2004), and Harold O. J. Brown's, *Heresies* (Garden City, NY: Doubleday Press, 1984). Brown refers to the crisis of 361 as 'The Second Stage of Arianism,' Ibid., p. 125.

29. The Nicene Council also failed to achieve the spiritual and geopolitical unity of the Empire that Constantine so desired. The spiritual and political factions between the west and east continued to debate one another over the issue of Christology. The eastern section of the Empire was influenced by Arianism, whereas, the western section of the Empire was influenced by the Athanasian/Nicene formula.

questions that were not understood easily by all parties concerned. Therefore, a trust factor (or lack thereof) contributed to the breach between east and west concerning the Trinity.

Basil's life

The aforementioned scenario reveals the nature and disposition of the church during the time of Basil. He entered the political and religious context of this time and by God's grace was able to address such challenging issues. Just as Arianism was moving into its second phase, God called a man to minister to the church and contribute to the discussion of Christ's person. In so doing, Basil helped the church understand the nature of the God it serves.

Basil was born in Caesarea of Cappadocia (modern Turkey) in the year 330, ten years after the pastor Arius and Bishop Alexander were engaged in a theological dispute over the status and nature of the Son within the Godhead. This debate was the focus of the Nicene Council (325). Athanasius, protégé of Alexander, and champion of the council, could be termed as one of the first generation of orthodox theologians. Basil, by virtue of his birth and life's calling is the second generation to advance the Nicene legacy of orthodoxy.

Education

Basil enjoyed the privileges of an admirable social standing. Philip Rousseau stated, 'Basil belonged to a relatively prosperous and locally prominent family in Pontus, near the Black Sea coast of Asia Minor.'[30] His family included four brothers and five sisters who embraced Christianity. Two of his brothers, Gregory of Nyssa and Peter of Sebaste, and his sister, Marcrina the Younger, were declared saints by the Eastern Orthodox Church (as was Basil). Their lineage was traced to the third century, 'to the disciples of Gregory Thaumaturgus, who had brought Christianity to Pontus

---

30.   Philip Rousseau, *Basil of Caesarea* (Los Angeles, CA: University of California Press, 1994), p. 1.

and had himself, so Basil believed, been a disciple of Origen.'[31] According to *The Catholic Encyclopedia*, the family suffered persecution under Maximus Galerius (305–14). During this time of persecution, Basil's immediate family was forced to live in the mountains near Pontus.[32]

Basil was educated under the direct tutelage of his father, St. Basil the Elder, who was a rhetorician. Basil's father died about 340 when Basil was at the tender age of ten. Consequently, he was sent to Caesarea to continue his studies. Haykin wrote that it was in Caesarea that 'he met and formed a lifelong friendship with Gregory of Nazianzus.'[33] From Caesarea, Basil studied at Constantinople with the celebrated Libanius (347). From there he traveled to Athens, which, according to Frances Young, was the 'leading university in the world.'[34] While at Athens his friendship with Gregory of Nazianzus flourished. Regarding his affinity to Athens, Gregory commented:

> For it brought me to know Basil more perfectly, though he had not been unknown to me before; and in my pursuit of letters, I attained happiness …We were contained by Athens, like two branches of some river-stream, for after leaving the common fountain of our fatherland, we had been separated in our varying pursuit of culture, and were now again united by the impulsion of God no less than by our one agreement.[35]

31. John Behr, *The Nicene Faith*, p. 263. Rousseau also concurred with Behr's assessment. Rousseau, *Basil of Caesarea*, p. 14.

32. Joseph McSorley, 'St. Basil the Great,' in *The Catholic Encyclopedia* (New York, NY: Robert Appleton Company 1907). Accessed online 8 July, 2009; available from http://www.newadvent.org/cathen/ This also is confirmed by Gregory of Nazianzus in *The Panegyric on St. Basil, Nicene and Post-Nicene Fathers*, eds. Philip Schaff and Henry Wace, vol. 7 (Peabody, MA: Hendrickson Publishers, 1994), p. 396.

33. Michael A. G. Haykin, *Rediscovering the Church Fathers* (Wheaton, IL: Crossway, 2011), p. 106.

34. Frances Young, *From Nicaea to Chalcedon* (Philadelphia, PA: Fortress Press, 1983), p. 93.

35. Gregory of Nazianzen, *The Panegyric on St. Basil, Nicene and Post-Nicene Fathers*, eds. Philip Schaff and Henry Wace, vol. 7 (Peabody, MA: Hendrickson Publishers, 1994), p. 400.

Apparently, Gregory remembered Athens fondly and his friendship with Basil was both deep and enduring.

The curriculum at Athens proved suitable to the keen mind of Basil. He studied ancient philosophy, astronomy, science, logic, grammar, and geometry. Yet, regardless of the advantages of the educational system at Athens, Basil was not happy. Rousseau stated:

> Rowdy divisions in the student body seem to have been promoted mainly by boisterous loyalty to individual teachers and sprang almost inevitably from the structure of the academic community... students were in practice, on their arrival, open market commodities; and rival gangs of established pupils attempted to capture, often by violence, further devotees for the masters they admired.[36]

Apparently, his five years at Athens (350-5) were not as pleasant as Gregory's stay at the city. Basil left in 355 and returned to Caesarea.

Family relations

Upon his return to Caesarea, Basil began teaching rhetoric, following his father's example. He excelled as a teacher and was comfortable in that role. However, his life changed through the verbal witness of his sister, Macrina. She challenged Basil to consider his relationship with God. Although his Christian family influenced him, it does not appear that Basil had embraced Christ as Savior. Macrina seemed to sense that Basil was very proud of himself. Yet to be fair to Basil, there is no doubt that, while at Athens, his conscience corrected him. However, he never made a public declaration that could be considered a salvation testimony. Thus, while living with his sister, she took the opportunity to witness to her famous brother, Basil.

---

36. Rousseau, *Basil of Caesarea*, p. 30.

Macrina

Macrina (327?–379) also was born in Cappadocia and was the eldest child of Basil the Elder and Emmelia. She was engaged to be married at the age of twelve (as was customary of the times) but her fiancé died before the marriage. She resolved to remain single basing her decision on the rationale that her engagement was the same as a marriage. Gregory of Nyssa stated, 'She persisted that the man who had been linked to her by her parents' arrangement was not dead, but that she considered him who lived to God, thanks to the hope of the resurrection, to be absent only, not dead; it was wrong not to keep faith with the bridegroom who was away.'[37]

Because of her decision, she devoted herself to the Lord, raising her younger brothers and sisters in the absence of her father who had died. With her father gone, Macrina accepted the role of caregiver along with her mother. This time allowed Macrina to develop a philosophical system of life that flowed naturally from Christianity. Macrina definitely was more Christian than philosopher as she did live a life of peace, which greatly affected her mother.[38] Her witness to her mother did not go unnoticed.

Tragedy was not far from the two women as Emmelia's young son, Naucratius, died from a hunting accident. Macrina's mother already had lost her husband and now a son. The emotional distress over the loss of her son overcame Emmelia to the point that she could not speak. The only person who could care for her mother was her eldest daughter Macrina, who nurtured and comforted her during this terrible calamity.

After the children left home (her sisters married and her brothers went to college), she and her mother formed a community of women who shared the same goals. This community seems to have been a development of an early form of monasticism as Macrina embraced

---

37. Gregory of Nyssa, *Life of Macrina*, translated by W. K. Lowther Clarke (London: Society for Promoting Christian Knowledge, 1916), p. 25.

38. For more information, see Anna Silvas' *Macrina the Younger: Philosopher of God* (London: Brepols Publishers, 2008).

a simple life (one without domestic servants), which included regular prayers and the singing of hymns.

Macrina and Basil

In his biography of Macrina, Gregory of Nyssa, gave insight into the relationship between Macrina and Basil. Gregory wrote:

> Macrina's brother, the great Basil, returned after his long period of education, already a practiced rhetorician. He was puffed up beyond measure with the pride of oratory and looked down on the local dignitaries, excelling in his own estimation all the men of leading and position. Nevertheless, Macrina took him in hand, and with such speed did she draw him toward the mark of philosophy that he forsook the glories of this world and despised fame gained by speaking, and deserted it for this busy life where one toils with one's hands. His renunciation of property was complete, lest anything should impede the life of virtue.[39]

Macrina seemed to have persuaded Basil to become a Christian even though his mind and emotions were contemplating philosophy and his career advancement. This may account for Basil's disdain for Athens. He simply was dealing with his relationship with the Lord at Athens and then encountered Christ at his home with the added influence of Macrina.

Upon his salvation, Basil received baptism by Dianius and subsequently was ordained *reader*[40] (meaning ordained to ministry) within the church. Soon he gave up his teaching career and embraced an ascetic lifestyle. This is a result of the direct influence of his godly sister, Macrina.

---

39. Gregory of Nyssa, 'The Life of St. Macrina,' in *Christian Classics Ethereal Library* (accessed online 25 May 2011), available from http://www.ccel.org.

40. *The Concise Oxford Dictionary of the Christian Church*, s.v. 'Lector/Reader.' This position was associated with a person who had embraced the ministry. Their assignment was to read Old Testament prophecies, the epistles, and in some places the Gospels.

Asceticism led Basil to Egypt, Palestine, Syria, and Mesopotamia.[41] Basil wrote that his desire was to study 'many men's cities and know many men's ways'.[42] One can assume that since he visited monasteries, his true desire was to understand and contemplate a life of devotion to the Lord.

Gregory of Nyssa

Gregory, the younger brother of Basil, was born in 335. He did not have the opportunity for education as did his older brother. In his letter to Libanius, Gregory stated that he was taught by Basil.[43] However, in spite of the fact that he never studied at a major university, he became proficient in the area of teaching rhetoric. His friend, Gregory of Nazianzus, chided him for his vocation as a rhetorician instead of being more committed to Christianity.[44]

Once again, it was the faithful witness of Macrina that impressed Gregory to contemplate '... the emptiness of worldly success and Gregory of Nazianzus attracted him to sacred studies and a life of prayer'.[45] His devotion to the Lord became the focal point of his life as he entered his brother's monastery at Pontus. While secluded at this beautiful location, he studied Origen. Yet the scenery of Pontus made a strong impression upon him as he reflected upon nature in several of his writings. For example, in his letter to Adelphius the Lawyer, he commented on the natural beauty of creation. He stated:

> The gifts bestowed upon the spot by Nature who beautifies the earth with unstudied grace are such as these: below the river

---

41. Young, *From Nicaea to Chalcedon*, p. 94.

42. Basil, *Letter 74.1*, trans. Blomfield Jackson, *NPNF*, vol. 8 (Peabody, MA: Hendrickson Publishers, 1994), p. 169.

43. Gregory of Nyssa, *Letter to Libanius* (EP 10), *NPNF*, 2nd series, vol. 5, p. 533.

44. Gregory of Nazianzen, *Letter to Gregory of Nyssa* (Ep 1), *NPNF* vol. 7 2nd series, p. 459.

45. Ronald E. Osborn, 'I'm Looking over a Four-leaf Clover that I Overlooked ...The Cappadocians Reconsidered,' *Impact* 8 (1982), pp. 22-3.

Halys makes the place fair to look upon with his banks, and gleams like a golden ribbon through their deep purple, reddening his current with soil he washes down. ... For forthwith vines, spread out over the slopes, and swellings, and hollows at the mountain's base, cover their color, like a green mantle, all the lower ground: and the season at this time even added to their beauty...[46]

Such were the ascetic thoughts of Gregory.

In the year 365, Basil joined Eusebius as co-pastor at the Metropolitan of Caesarea in Cappadocia. This team worked against the formidable challenge of the second phase of Arianism. The Arian bishops had the support of Emperor Valens, as he was sympathetic to the Arian cause. After five years, and at the death of Eusebius, Basil became sole bishop of Caesarea. The threat of Arianism, which was ever present, prompted Basil to persuade his brother, Gregory, to take the bishopric of Nyssa in 372. This move was an attempt to counter Emperor Valens' desire to divide Cappadocia into smaller districts.

Gregory was not suitable as a pastor in the beginning of his ministry as he began to make decisions that had disastrous consequences. John Behr suggested that Gregory convened a synod at Ancyra 'to achieve some kind of rapprochement with the disciples of Marcellus in Ancyra.'[47] Two years later, Gregory was accused of financial mismanagement, irregularities concerning his ordination, and general incompetence. Subsequently, he was banished from his bishopric.

There is no doubt that Gregory was more suited to theological contemplation than pastoral ministry, where conflict is a part of a pastor's life. Gregory was a gentle person who was thrown into the midst of conflict and he did not have the experience to resolve the problems he encountered. Tending the sheep and pasturing the flock is a learned skill that, at this point in time,

---

46.   Gregory of Nyssa, *Letter to Adelphius*, *NPNF*, vol. 5, p. 539.

47.   Behr, *The Nicene Faith*, vol. 2, part 2, p. 410.

Gregory did not possess. Basil commented that his brother was 'quite inexperienced in ecclesiastical affairs.'[48]

The Emperor Valens died in 378, which allowed Gregory to return to Nyssa. However, the event that catapulted Gregory into prominence was the death of his beloved brother Basil in the year 379. Eventually, Gregory did gain experience in ecclesiastical affairs. He attended the Council of Antioch in 379. Upon his return, he visited Macrina, who was on her deathbed. During this time of life, Gregory began to write extensively. He wrote *On Virginity*, *On the Creation of Man*, and one of his more famous works, *Against Eunomius*, that defended Basil's position against Eunomius. The impact of *Against Eunomius* is considerable. Jerome heard this work at the second ecumenical Council of Constantinople in May 381. For the next fifteen years, Gregory became a statesman/theologian presiding over the affairs of the church, conducting funerals of the imperial court (the infant princess Pulcheria and Empress Flaccilla). Very little is known about the latter years of Gregory's life. However, he went to be with the Lord in the year 395.

---

48.   Basil, *Letter 215*, NPNF, 2nd series, vol. 8, p. 255.

2

CONVERSION AND THEOLOGY

Salvation

The year was A.D. 355 when Basil returned to Caesarea to teach rhetoric, which meant that he followed in his father's footsteps. For nearly a year, he stayed at Caesarea teaching students, including his brother Gregory. In all likelihood, Basil molded his brother in the art of rhetoric, which may have been the catalyst for propelling Gregory into a secular career.

The year 356 proved to be a turning point in Basil's life as he came under the influence of Macrina, whose testimony was instrumental in his salvation. Soon after his baptism, he entered the ministry as an ordained reader.

> **Reader:** Due to the illiteracy of the members of the early church, some of the more literate Christians were instituted as a reader or lector. Their responsibility was to read certain portions of Scripture during the service. The reader was a minor position and often considered the first step towards entering the clergy or ministry.

Basil reflected upon his pre-conversion life in a letter to Eustathius of Sebaste. Basil stated:

> Much time had I spent in vanity, and had wasted nearly all my youth in the vain labor which I underwent in acquiring the wisdom

made foolish by God. Then once upon a time, like a man roused from deep sleep, I turned my eyes to the marvelous light of truth of the Gospel, and I perceived the uselessness of 'the wisdom of the princes of this world, that come to naught.' I wept many tears over my miserable life, and I prayed that guidance might be vouchsafed me to admit me to the doctrines of true religion.[1]

Interestingly, Basil described his former way of life as wasted and underscored his new life as embracing the light of truth. Later in life, he described the act of conversion as being a gift of the Holy Spirit whose purpose is to give the gift of life. Basil was adamant that the Holy Spirit 'searches even the depths of God, but the creature receives enlightenment concerning ineffable truths through the Spirit. He gives life together with the Father who enlivens all things, and with the life-giving Son.'[2] For Metropolitan Georges Khodr, Basil's understanding of the spiritual life centered upon the Scriptures. Regarding Basil, Khodr stated:

Basil affirms that all initiative belongs to God. By His love, the Trinitarian God makes His dwelling place within the human heart that is willing to receive Him. According to this view, that stresses divine initiative, no method or technique of the spiritual life can be considered important in itself. Divine grace bestows its gifts freely, and man is merely the receptacle who receives them with wonder.[3]

1. Asceticism

Basil followed Eustathius to Syria, Mesopotamia, Palestine, and Egypt during the year 357. While on this trip, he witnessed asceticism through monasticism as a way of viable Christianity.[4]

---

1. Basil, *Letter 223. 2, Nicene and Post-Nicene Fathers*, 2nd Series, vol. 8, p. 263.

2. Basil, *On the Holy Spirit* (Crestwood, NY: St. Vladimir's Press, 1980), p. 88.

3. Metropolitan Georges Khodr, 'Basil the Great: Bishop and Pastor,' *St. Vladimir's Theological Quarterly* 29 (Jan. 1985), pp. 15-16.

4. F. L. Cross and E. A. Livingstone, *The Oxford Dictionary of the Christian Church*, 3rd ed. (Oxford: Oxford University Press, 1997), s.v. 'Asceticism' is defined as 'moral training, often with the connotation of voluntary abstention from certain pleasures. It denotes (1) practices employed to combat vices and develop virtues and (2) the renunciation of various facets of customary social life and comfort, and the adoption of painful conditions for religious reasons.'

Asceticism was a means of obtaining purity before God. In the modern Evangelical world, the concept of holiness and sanctification could be thought of in the same realm. The ascetic way of life was a method of renouncing the vices of a Roman society that was morally bankrupt.[5] Yet, Paul Fedwick further stated, 'Basil, with other Christians, took refuge in the asceticism which emerged as a force in opposition to the secularized and Arianized church.'[6] Michael Haykin confirmed this when he stated, '...since the toleration of Christianity by Constantine many were now flocking into the church for base motives...'[7]

Amid growing secularism, the church that had embraced Arianism appeared to be struggling to develop converts, not to mention the difficulty of discipling new believers in the orthodox faith. The rationale for embracing an ascetic lifestyle primarily was discipleship and growth, although it also allowed for theological development that resulted in the ability to counter the arguments of the Arian bishops who denounced orthodox doctrine. However, asceticism was no mere political movement. Robert Wilken commented, 'The Fathers were convinced that men could not live a life of virtue in the world unless they regularly set themselves apart and cultivated the inner life. The life of a good man must be a life lived in fellowship with God.'[8] Therefore, since Arianism had engulfed the teaching of the church, the viable response was to separate from the unorthodox teaching, retreat to a place for solitude, and engage the Lord in order to conduct a ministry to the church.

---

5.   Chapter Three will address Basil's asceticism and monasticism in more detail. This chapter simply gives the historical overview so that the reader can begin to grasp the timeline of Basil's life and work.

6.   Paul Jonathan Fedwick, *The Church and the Charisma of Leadership in Basil of Caesarea* (Toronto: Pontifical Institute of Medieval Studies, 1979), p. 37.

7.   Michael A.G. Haykin, 'Defending the Holy Spirit's Deity: Basil of Caesarea, Gregory of Nyssa, and the Pneumatomachian Controversy of the 4th Century,' *Southern Baptist Seminary Journal of Theology* 7.3 (Fall 2003), pp. 74-5.

8.   Robert L. Wilken, 'The Spirit of Holiness: Basil of Caesarea and Early Christian Spirituality,' *Worship* 42:2 (Fall 1968), p. 85.

Asceticism, Arianism, and the church

One should recognize that the issue of Arianism in the church is not dismissed easily by the modern political method of appealing to the separation of church and state. In the fourth century, with the conversion of Constantine, the imperial ruler was able to impose upon the church political controls in religious affairs.[9] Therefore, if the imperial ruler favored Arianism then the church adopted his position. Against this background is where Basil sought the company of godly men and the ascetic lifestyle. His sole purpose was to live his life in such a way that he would encounter the blessings of God. The modern pastor should find encouragement in the model of Basil as he knew that denouncing orthodox doctrine would negate the blessings of God and thereby destroy one's ministry.

After his monastic trip with Eustathius, Basil returned to Pontus at the family estate of Annisa in the hope of joining his mother and sister in the ascetic way of life. However, Basil crossed the Iris River and founded his own community primarily to seek solace. He tried to convince his friend Gregory of Nazianzus to join him in the endeavor at Pontus. Basil wrote to Gregory of his concern that '...man's mind when distracted by his countless worldly cares cannot focus itself distinctly on the truth.'[10] Eventually, Gregory did join Basil for approximately one year. They worked on the *Philocalia* which is 'an anthology of Origen's works...'[11] Rousseau attributed his interest in Origen to his travels east and primarily to the city of Alexandria where he would 'discover not only the memory but also the surviving writings of Origen, and probably of his famous contemporaries and students.'[12]

The *Philocalia* was instrumental in giving Basil the advantage in his debates with the Arians. The ancient church historian

---

9. See Chapter 1.

10. Basil, *Letter 2*, translated by Roy J. Deferrari, 4 vols. (New York, NY: G. P. Putnam's Sons, 1926), 1:9.

11. Mark DelCogliano, *Introduction to the Work Against Eunomius* (Washington: The Catholic University of America Press, 2011), p. 9.

12. Philip Rousseau, *Basil of Caesarea*, p. 83.

Socrates Scholasticus stated, '... after a careful perusal of the writings of that great man [Origen], they contend against the Arians with manifest advantage.'[13] Rousseau commented that the *Philocalia* revealed 'Origen addressing directly the problem of how to argue the Christian case against non-believers. They concern the purpose of apologetic and focus on the issues that were likely to cause pagans difficulty.'[14] The importance of the study of Origen is that it helped shape Basil's theology and, thus, propelled him to defend the orthodox doctrine against the Arians.[15]

Theological development

In the late 350s, the Emperor Constantius sympathized with the Arian party and subsequently called a series of councils in order to bring unity to the church via Arianism. These councils met during the years 357–9 and re-established Arianism as an ecclesiastical and political force within the church.[16]

Homoiousios phase

The definition of the word *homoiousios* is 'of like or similar substance.'[17] The aftermath of the Council of Nicea left open the

13. Socrates Scholasticus, *Church History Book IV, 26* (NPNF 2nd series vol. 2), p. 111. This is a reference to the debates between Basil and Eunomius. Interestingly, the theological advantage was Basil's because of his study at his monastic community on the banks of the Iris River.

14. Rousseau, *Basil of Caesarea*, p. 84.

15. Socrates Scholasticus stated, 'When the defenders of Arianism quoted the same author (Origen) in confirmation, as they imagined, of their own views, these two (Basil and Gregory) confuted them, and clearly proved that their opponents did not at all understand the reasoning of Origen' (page 111 – see footnote 13).

16. The councils alluded to are the Council of Sirmium, Council of Seleucia, and Rimini. Basically, these councils gave strength to the Semi-Arian position *that the Son was like the Father.* Hence, it is the middle position between the Arians, who denied the Son was like or even similar to the Father and the orthodoxy of the Nicene formula which stated that the Son has the same substance as the Father. The council at Sirmium banned the use of *homoousios* and *homoiousios*. In other words, the ban was directed at the orthodox language of Nicea. These councils produced the *Dated Creed.*

17. G. W. H. Lampe, *A Patristic Greek Lexicon* (Oxford: Clarendon Press, 1961), s.v. 'homoiousios.'

possibility that the Arians could emerge with an emperor who favored them. As previously stated, that emperor was Constantius.

The result was that the second phase[18] of Arianism began to emerge in the 350s primarily with Eunomius.[19]

The problematic issue with Eunomius was that he utilized Neoplatonic language to describe the nature of God. In doing so, he emphasized that the Father was the cause (since he is ingenerate) of the Son (who is made or generated) from the Father but of a different substance than the Father. Eunomius wrote, 'Wherefore if the Word of God demonstrates that his Will is his Operation, and not that his Substance is such, and that the Only-Begotten subsisted by the Will of the Father; 'tis necessary that the Son preserve this Likeness, not as to substance but as to Operation, which is also his Will.'[20]

> **Neoplatonism:** This is the philosophical system of Plato revived and revised by Plotinus. The basic tenets of Neoplatonic thought centre upon the doctrine of three hypostases: The One, who is the ultimate and unknowable source from which everything derives its existence; The Intelligence, which is the realm of perfect knowledge; and the Soul, which is thought and activity. In its basic form, this philosophical approach to the knowledge of God was incompatible with Christianity. The Incarnation was at odds with the hypostasis of The One. The Incarnation ensures the knowability of God, which is in opposition to the basic tenet of Neo-platonism. Gradually, philosophical studies begin to impact Christianity to the extent that theologians such as Origen, Augustine, and Dionysius were heavily influenced by Neoplatonic thought.

The basic issue that Eunomius tried to teach is that the substance of the Son is different from the Father's substance. The Son has this different substance because the will of the Father

---

18. See Chapter 1 for an overview of the Arian Crisis.

19. For Eunomius, see his work, *First Apology*.

20. Eunomius, *First Apology*, p. 24.

.generated him. For Eunomius, the Son was created in the 'likeness' of the Father but not of the same substance as the Father. John Behr stated that Eunomius understood the Son as 'the product of the will of God and is, therefore, as temporal as the activity that brought him into being: before being begotten or created he was not.'[21] Eunomius not only revived Arianism, but he also became, for all practical purposes, the backbone of the second phase of Arianism. In an interesting note of this period, Jerome made this famous statement, 'The whole world groaned and was astonished to find itself Arian.'[22] Thus, with the approval of the Emperor and the vote of councils, Arianism was a force to be recognized and addressed.

> **Eunomius:** He was bishop at Cyzicus in Mysia and student of Aetius. His primary work was *First Apology* in which he propagated the claims that the Son did not have the same substance as the Father. Basil responded to this work with *Against Eunomius*. In A.D. 378, Eunomius wrote a three-volume work entitled, *Second Apology,* to which Gregory of Nyssa responded with his *Against Eunomius.* Eunomius denied the generation of the Son but taught that the Son was immediately created by the Father. The Father then gave the Son created power, which allowed the Son to resemble the Father but not in substance. His views were not widely accepted and after the Council of Constantinople, in 381, they simply were no longer a factor.

Basil's ministry was related directly to the second phase of Arianism. His time and place in history allowed him to be the focal point of renewed orthodoxy. However, Basil did not start with the Nicene formula. His theological studies not only took him on the journey to embrace the orthodox position but allowed him to become one of the able champions for and contributors to the orthodox position.

In 359 or 360, Basil left his ascetical retreat to attend a church synod at Constantinople. He was moving toward a gradual

---

21. Behr, *The Nicene Faith*, vol. 2, part 2, p. 280.

22. Jerome, *The Dialogue against the Luciferians*, 19 (NPNF 2nd series vol. 6), p. 329.

involvement with the conflicts taking place in the church. However, it should be noted that by this time Basil was ordained to the ministry. Therefore, it does seem as if his awareness of the Arian conflict is related directly to his emerging role as a minister. As Basil prepared for the role of minister-theologian, he turned to his friend Apollinarius for theological matters.

The correspondence with Apollinarius revealed the theological insights of Basil. In the *Letter 362* (to Apollinarius), Basil 'reveals himself to be a homoiousian theologian'.[23] Basil wrote:

> Those authors of universal confusion who have filled the world with arguments and speculations have rejected the term 'substance' [*ousia*] as foreign to the divine oracles; so please show us in what sense the fathers used it and whether you have not ever found it in standing with the Scriptures ... Next please give us full discussion of the actual homoiousion, as I believe this is the object of the maneuvers – they are making a dead set at 'substance' so as to leave no opening for 'consubstantial.' What meaning does it bear?[24]

This inquiry reveals that Basil was eager to learn more about the terminology that directed the study of Trinitarian thought. He appealed to Apollinarius because of the confusing language of Eunomius (hence the reference to 'authors of universal confusion'). However, Basil revealed his own understanding of the Trinity. He stated:

> Our own idea is this. Whatever one takes the substance of the Father to be in basic reality, one is entirely bound to take the substance of the Son to be that too ... *But it seems to me that the expression 'undeviating similar' fits such a notion better than 'of one substance'* [italics added for emphasis]. I feel that one light displaying no difference of greater or less intensity from another

---

23. Stephen M. Hildebrand, *The Trinitarian Theology of Basil of Caesarea* (Washington, D.C.: The Catholic University of America Press, 2007), p. 37.

24. G. L. Prestige, *St. Basil the Great and Apollinaris of Laodicea* (London: S.P.C.K., 1956), p. 38.

light is not 'the same,' since each consists in a particular deter-
minate substance, but should rightly be described as precisely
undeviatingly similar in substance.[25]

The emphasis of Basil is that the 'like without a difference' (apar-
allaktos homoios) seems to explain the relationship between the
Father and Son. The analogy he used to clarify his position is
that 'light is not the same' but similar in substance.

At this point in his ministry, Basil began to think theologically. He perceived that the Council of Constantinople was a loss
for the homoiousian party as they adopted the Homoian Creed.[26]
Consequently, Basil left the council and returned to Caesarea.
However, on a personal level, this council was a turning point
for Basil. 'This Council of Constantinople marks the beginning
of Basil's life as a Cappadocian cleric and his entrée into the
wider ecclesiastical world and its conflicts.'[27]

> **Homoian Creed:** This creed was adopted by the Council of Constantinople
> of A.D. 360. The council was attended by two opposing factions, neither
> of which were orthodox in their respective positions. The first party was
> the heteroousians, who declared the Son to be of a different substance
> than the Father. The second party were the homoiousians, who adhered to
> the premise that the Son was like the Father according to the Scriptures.
> The debate was actually victorious for the heteroousians but Constantius
> banished Aetius, which threw the debate and final victory in favor of the
> homoiousians. Subsequently, this small council adopted the position that the
> Son was like the Father but not the same as the Father.

While at Caesarea, Basil learned that Dianius was coerced
by imperial threats to capitulate to the Homoian Creed.
Nonetheless, Basil interpreted Dianius' actions as a strong denial

---

25. Prestige, St. Basil the Great and Apollinaris of Laodicea, p. 39.

26. This creed prohibited the use of ousia and hypostasis.

27. Mark DelCogliano, Introduction to the Work against Eunomius (Washington: The
    Catholic University of America Press, 2011), p. 11.

of the Nicene Orthodox Creed he once professed. He retreated to Annisa and engaged in asceticism for a period of two years. In 362, Gregory joined him again, but by mid-year Gregory left and Basil went back to Caesarea. This year was significant in that Basil did reconcile with Dianius before the latter died and he reverenced his pastor's memory in later years.[28]

Homoousios phase

Basil continued on his journey towards orthodoxy. The year was 362 and he found himself in the midst of rethinking his theological position. A panoramic view of his life and ministry is in order to understand his journey towards Trinitarian orthodoxy. During the second part of 362, Basil was an ordained minister preparing for his role as a future pastor. However, Basil was not only concerned for his local ministry but he entered the Arian debate with the work, *Against Eunomius.* This work was written in approximately 362–3[29] to refute Eunomius' work entitled *First Apology.*[30] One of the more interesting features of the work was that Basil seemed to admit that *Against Eunomius* was his first theological attempt. Basil stated:

> So, on account of Your Charity, who enjoins us to do this, and for the sake of our own well being, it is necessary for us to accept the responsibility of allying ourselves with the truth and refuting this falsehood. Giving no heed to our weakness for this task and although *we are altogether untrained in such a form of speaking,* [italics added for emphasis] we undertake this task insofar as the Lord apportions us knowledge to us.[31]

---

28. DelCogliano, *Introduction to the Work against Eunomius*, p. 12.

29. The dating system followed is that of G. L. Prestige, *St. Basil the Great and Apollinaris of Laodicea* (London: S.P.C.K., 1956), pp. 7-37.

30. See Footnote 8.

31. Basil, *Against Eunomius,* translated by Mark DelCogliano and Andrew Raddle-Gallwitz (Washington, D.C.: The Catholic University of America Press, 2011), pp. 81-2.

If Basil alluded to *Against Eunomius* as being his first work, then it revealed something of his journey or transitional development as a theologian.

Against Eunomius revealed that Basil was thinking through the implications of the Nicene formula and particularly the word *homoousios*. Stephen Hildebrand stated, 'Basil used *homoousios* only once in a theological sense which indicates at the very least that *homoousios* has not achieved the status of a "watchword" and at most that Basil is still uncomfortable with the term.'[32] *Against Eunomius* not only revealed that Basil was moving away from the *homoiousios* phase but that he calculated the Nicene formula (*homoousios*) without a full acceptance of it.

Another interesting feature of *Against Eunomius* is that the work reveals the beginning stages of Basil's development of his Trinitarian theological contribution. *Against Eunomius* presents the concept that substance (*hypostasis*) is a synonym for being (*ousia*). When referring to the relationship between the Father and Son, Basil quoted Hebrews 1:3, using the term hypostasis to mean substance in the typical biblical sense of the word. He stated, 'For it has been spoken of ... the "imprint of the substance" (*character tns hypostasis*, Heb 1.3), in order that we be taught the consubstantial (*ton homoousion*).'[33]

The argument is predicated upon the fact that substance (*hypostasis*) is a synonym for being (*ousia*), which means that the Son has the same substance as the Father. Hildebrand concurred when he wrote:

They are largely synonymous except that the connotation

> **hypostasis**: This Greek word refers to 'essence' or 'substance.' It denotes real, personal subsistence. Thus when referring to the Trinity, the individual members possessed a hypostasis or individual subsistence. The members had a personal existence as part of the one undivided essence.

---

32. Stephen M. Hildebrand, *The Trinitarian Theology of Basil of Caesarea* (Washington, D.C.: The Catholic University of America Press, 2007), p. 45.

33. Lucian Turcescu, 'Prosopon and Hypostasis in Basil of Caesarea's "Against Eunomius" and the Epistles,' *Vigiliae Christianae* 51:4 (1997), p. 377.

of *hypostasis* stresses actual real existence as opposed to concep-
tual or merely mental existence. Here *hypostasis* is not opposed
to *einai* (*ousia*) or distinguished from it, but simply emphasizes
an aspect of it – its real existence ... Thus, hypostasis here simply
means 'really existing thing'.[34]

The theological characteristic of *Against Eunomius* revealed that,
at the time of writing, Basil did not reject *homoousios* in totality,
but allowed a more cautious, yet limited, acceptance or tolerance
of the word. In so doing, he cognitively moved away from the
rigid *homoiousios* position.

An additional interesting feature of the work is that Eunomius
used the term 'begotten' (*agennetos*) to refer to God's essence (*ousia*).
Basil wrote, 'As a matter of fact, by adding: "rather, that his unbegottenness is unbegotten substance," Eunomius indicated that unbegottenness is precisely what God is.'[35] Eunomius wrongly concluded
that since the Son was begotten (*agennetos*) he could not be God.
Basil stated that Eunomius committed blasphemy. He wrote, 'Since
he [Eunomius] wants to show that the only-begotten Son and God is
unlike the God and Father, he keeps silent about the names of "Father" and "Son", and simply discusses the "unbegotten" and "begotten." He conceals names that belong to the saving faith and hands
over doctrines of his blasphemy unveiled.'[36] Basil's response was to
identify 'unbegottenness' as a property only of the Father that is not
shared by all three members of the Godhead. Basil stated:

> For example the divinity is common, whereas, fatherhood and
> sonship are distinguishing marks: from the combination of both,
> that is, of the common and unique, we arrive at comprehension
> of the truth. Consequently, upon hearing 'unbegotten light' we
> think of the Father, whereas upon hearing 'begotten light' we
> receive the notion of the Son.[37]

---

34. Hildebrand, *The Trinitarian Theology*, p. 59.

35. Basil, *Against Eunomius*, translated by Mark DelCogliano and Andrew Raddle-Gallwitz (Washington, D.C.: The Catholic University of America Press, 2011), p. 95.

36. Basil, *Against Eunomius*, pp. 115-16.

37. Ibid., p. 175.

By understanding that each member of the Trinity has specific and unique properties, Basil began to formulate the differences between each member. However, it should be noted that he positively claimed that each member not only shared divinity but rather each was divine in their nature. *Against Eunomius* revealed Basil as a 'budding theologian' beginning to emerge as a theological force within the fourth-century ecclesiastical debates.

The year 364 proved to be a theologically productive one for Basil. *Letter 9* was written to Maximus concerning the writings of Dionysius. The content of the correspondence surrounds Dionysius. However, Basil seized the opportunity to reveal that he embraced the Nicene position. The letter revealed that he accepted the language of Nicea as he preferred the term *homoousios*. Basil stated:

> If I must give my own view, it is this. The phrase 'like in essence,' if it be read with the addition 'without any difference,' I accept as conveying the same sense as homoousion, in accordance with the sound meaning of homoousion ... If, then the phrase be accepted in this sense, I have no objection to it. But if anyone cuts off the qualification 'without any difference' from the word 'like,' as was done at Constantinople, then I regard the phrase with suspicion, as derogatory to the dignity of the Only-begotten.[38]

The letter definitely revealed that Basil preferred the language of Nicea. In fact, the point of the letter was Basil's critique of Dionysius's work. Basil believed that Dionysius goes too far and admitted to a substance.[39]

The reference to 'Constantinople' reveals a timeline that should be considered.[40] This is a reference to the Council of Constantinople held in the year 360. The time of the letter was, obviously, after the council, which would require a date of 361

---

38. Basil, *Letter 9*, (*NPNF* 2nd series vol. 8), p. 123.

39. Ibid.

40. Basil, *Letter 9*, p. 123.

or later. Keeping that in mind, Prestige's work becomes invaluable. Prestige argued for the dating of *Letter 361* and possibly *Letter 362* being in the same year as the Council of Seleucia, which is 359. Assuming the dates are correct, the theological chronology of Basil's journey to theological orthodoxy is as follows:

359 – He questions the meaning of *homoousios* while preferring the term *homoiousios*.

362–363 – He tolerates the use of *homoousios* as demonstrated in *Against Eunomius*.

364 – Later he accepts *homoousios* as depicted in his *Letter 9*.

The rationale of Prestige is that Basil had inquired about the meaning of *homoousios* (359). He then tolerated the usage of it in his work, *Against Eunomius* (362–3). Finally, he accepted the term with given qualifications as stated in *Letter 9*. This means his conversion to *homoousios* would have occurred during the year 364.

Hypostasis phase

The fact that Basil used the word *hypostasis* in *Against Eunomius* suggests that he was thinking through the theological implications of the word. In Book 3 of *Against Eunomius*, Basil actually used *hypostasis* in the technical manner in which it would become known. He stated, 'So, then, if holiness is the Spirit's nature, as it is for the Father and Son, how does he have a nature that is third and foreign to theirs? I think that Isaiah recorded the Seraphim crying 'Holy!' three times for this reason: because holiness in nature is observed in three subsistences.'[41] The idea Basil communicated was that there are three substances being worshiped in the Isaiah passage. Thus, Basil was beginning, in some sense, to identify substance (*hypostasis*) with individual personhood. However, the tech-

---

41. Basil, *Against Eunomius 3.3*. The word 'subsistences' is translated from the Greek word *hypostasis*.

nical sense of hypostasis was not developed until a more serious threat was addressed.

Bishop Basil

In 370, Basil was elected Bishop of Caesarea. As the new Bishop, his immediate challenge and goal was to unify the eastern and western church.[42] This meant that he must come to a resolution regarding the doctrine of the Trinity.[43] The problem he addressed was the second phase of Arianism that logically turned toward the deity of the Holy Spirit. In other words, one might ask, 'How is the Holy Spirit related to the Godhead?' or 'Is the Holy Spirit God?'

In order to grasp the theological issues of the late 360s and early 370s, a brief review will be provided. The issue of Jesus Christ's divinity did not subside. Arianism had made a strong reappearance under Constantius. However, the theological question simply progressed to include the third member of the Trinity, the Holy Spirit. Therefore, in order to bring theological consensus to the church, Basil needed to address the main point of division that existed among the bishops – the inner relationship among the members of the Trinity!

Marcellus

Marcellus was a main proponent of orthodoxy at the Nicene Council (325). He took a strong stand against the Arians. However, that does not mean that he took a positive stand in favor of the Nicene Creed.[44] Basil believed that Marcellus taught the tenets of Sabellius, who concluded that there was no eternal

---

42. Joseph T. Lienhard, 'Basil of Caesarea, Marcellus of Ancyra, and Sabellius,' *Church History* 58:2 (June 1989), p. 159.

43. A more detailed account of the Trinitarian problem will be addressed in a later chapter. This chapter is providing a historical overview of Basil's life and his ecclesiastical and theological contributions.

44. Lienhard stated that in 'the extant fragments of the *Contra Asterium* Marcellus never mentions the Council of Nicea, its creed, or the word *homoousion.*' see 'Basil of Caesarea, Marcellus of Ancyra, and Sabellius,' *Church History* 58:2 (June 1989), p. 160.

distinction within the Trinity. Therefore, the terms Father, Son, and Holy Spirit do not correspond to different persons but rather as a reference to the one God existing in three different modes.[45] However, Marcellus was not a pure Sabellian as Basil proposed. Marcellus understood that there was a distinction between the members of the Trinity. Regarding Marcellus's proclamation, J.N.D. Kelly noted:

> This externalization of the Logos does not, of course, result in His becoming a second hypostasis; His coming forth or procession is described as an extension or expansion of the Monad, which at creation and the incarnation become, without undergoing any division, a dyad, and with the outpouring of the Spirit a triad ... Further, although he [Marcellus] lacked language and even concepts to express the distinction, he envisaged the pre-existent Logos as somehow other than the indivisible spirit with Whom He was nevertheless, one and the same.[46]

Marcellus' thought was not unorthodox per se. The question should be asked, 'Why did Basil think that Marcellus was a Sabellian?' Perhaps the answer would be that Marcellus, regardless of his defense of orthodoxy at Nicea, became over-zealous in his defense of Christology, thereby developing a system that allowed the charge of Modalism to be leveled against him by his critics.

An additional issue should be examined as aforementioned. The agenda of Basil to unite the eastern and western church cannot be dismissed readily from consideration. In order to unite the east and west, Marcellus' influence must be diminished. Again, Lienhard acknowledged the various interpretative differences within Christianity. The Patriarchal Sees were theologically distinct from one another. He stated:

---

45. A clarification of terms is necessary: The *Sabellians* and the *Arians* are two different parties who basically asked the same question about the relationship within the Trinity. The Arians focused upon the Son, whereas, the Sabellians, of the latter fourth century, focused upon the Holy Spirit.

46. J. N. D. Kelly, *Early Christian Doctrines* (San Francisco, CA: Harper Collins Publishing, 1978), p. 241.

Rome, and the entire West, had never condemned Marcellus as a heretic. On the contrary, Pope Julius had received him into communion in 340 or 341. Antioch was divided among three bishops: Euzios, the 'Arian'; Meletius, whom Basil fervently supported and who had been in exile since 370; and Paulinus, whom the conservative Lucifer of Cagliari had ordained in 362 and whom many Westerners favored ... Constantinople, while not yet a patriarchate, was the capital city; its bishop was the 'Arian' Demophilus.[47]

Basil, as the newly appointed bishop, tried to seize the opportunity to unite the Latin west with the Greek east and, therefore, secure a united Christian church throughout the Roman Empire.

If Basil was trying to unite the church and his strategy was to win the west by condemning Marcellus, it was a miscalculated strategy. His thoughts must have been that in order to unite the eastern and western church, Marcellus would need to be condemned by the west so that the east would be accepting of the western tradition. Basil underestimated the influence of Marcellus, as he was well known in the west. One of his more infamous relationships was with the legendary champion of Nicea, Athanasius.

Marcellus, Athanasius, and Basil
In 343, the Synod of Sardica revealed an example of the popularity of Marcellus and Athanasius in the west. Emperor Constans called the synod to try to unite the eastern and western churches. The problem was the synod never convened as a whole party representing both sides. Lienhard stated, 'The Westerners wanted Athanasius and Marcellus seated, a move the Easterners could not agree to, since they held that both of them had been validly deposed; so the Easterners withdrew to Philippopolis. The western synod of Sardica reinforced the sense of party unity

---

47.   Lienhard, 'Basil of Caesarea, Marcellus of Ancyra, and Sabellius,' pp. 160-1.

and hardened the spirit of opposition.'[48] The synod affirmed the theology of Athanasius and Marcellus as the encyclical letter 'regularly linked the names of Athanasius and Marcellus'.[49]

Although the western Synod of Sardica vindicated both Athanasius and Marcellus, the relationship between both men was strained. After the council, Athanasius broke communion with Marcellus because of the latter's association with Bishop Photinus. This fracture in the relationship between Marcellus and Athanasius was well known. Basil may have been thinking that the west was ready to consider Marcellus who did not have the support of Athanasius. However, Basil did not consider the fact that Athanasius never condemned Marcellus.

From 346 to 361 there is no record of the activity of Marcellus. In 362, he does appear in Antioch. The See at Antioch and Marcellus set the stage for ecclesiastical events as there were two parties claiming the right to the bishopric of Antioch: the Eustathians and the Meletians.[50] The schism of Antioch meant that there were two rival bishops and Marcellus was in communion with Paulinus, the leader of the Eustathians. The significance of the Antioch schism is twofold. First, Athanasius sent a letter trying to unite the Eustathians with the Meletians. He recognized that these two groups were actually the same theologically in that both parties adhered to the Nicene tradition. Furthermore, Athanasius had approved Paulinus as the true Bishop of Antioch, which allowed Paulinus to send representatives to Athanasius asking for his help in reconciling the two groups. Second, Basil's plan to unite the eastern and western factions was to support Meletius in this ecclesiastical power struggle. Again,

---

48. Joseph T. Lienhard, *Contra Marcellum: Marcellus of Ancyra and Fourth-Century Theology* (Washington, D.C.: The Catholic University of America Press, 1999), p. 6.

49. Ibid.

50. Hildebrand, *The Trinitarian Theology of Basil of Caesarea* (Washington, DC: The Catholic University of America Press, 2007), p. 85, states that there were 'no fewer than four men who claimed possession of the see: Paulinus, the old-Nicene disciple of Eustathius; Meletius, whom Basil supported; Euzoius, an 'Arian'; and Vitalis, an Apollinarian.'

according to Lienhard, 'In Basil's mind, the one thing that would unite Athanasius and the Westerners with himself and the Meletians at Antioch was the condemnation of Marcellus. In 371, Basil tried to drive a wedge between Athanasius and Marcellus by having Athanasius repudiate Marcellus.'[51]

> **Meletians:** These were followers of Meletius who had disagreed with the larger church at Alexandria over treatment of the *lapsi*. The *lapsi* were Christians who, under persecution, recanted their testimony or even handed over the Scriptures in order to avoid further ill-treatment. After the Edict of Milan, the *lapsi* were allowed to re-enter the church with full fellowship. Meletius wanted stricter sanctions against the *lapsi*. His followers became known as Meletians and propagated martyrdom as the price of total allegiance to the Lord.

In order to accomplish this plan, he had to appeal to Athanasius. The appeal to Athanasius would mean: (1) the west would denounce Marcellus, thus giving Basil the support of Athanasius and his influence in the west along with the Egyptian churches, and (2) Antioch, under the leadership of Meletius, could help Basil lead the east to forge a truce with the west to unify the church doctrinally.

Basil sent six letters to appeal to Athanasius to denounce Marcellus.[52] *Letter 66* depicted Basil's concern for unity among the eastern and western churches. He stated:

> I, for my part, have long been aware, so far as my moderate intelligence has been able to judge of current events, that the one way of safety for the Churches of the East lies in having the sympathy of the bishops of the West. For if only those bishops liked to show the same energy on behalf of the Christians sojourning in our part of the world which they have shown in the case of one or two of the men convicted of breaches of

---

51. Lienhard, *Contra Marcellum*, p. 8.

52. *Letters 61, 66, 67, 69 80, 82* were written in the year 371.

orthodoxy in the West, our common interests would probably
reap no small benefit, our sovereigns treating the authority of the
people with respect, and the laity in all quarters unhesitatingly
following them.[53]

The goal of Basil was to seek unity but he attempted to do so in
a harsh manner. Marcellus was problematic in his doctrine but
he did stand for the Nicene orthodox faith. Regardless of that
fact, Basil did not recognize the historical issues involved and
pursued his plan.

In *Letter 67*, Basil asked Athanasius to support Meletius as
Bishop of Antioch. He stated, 'My object was to make it plain
that the sections, now divided into several parts, ought to be
united under the God-beloved Meletius.'[54] In *Letter 69*, he asked
Athanasius to consult with Rome in order to 'exterminate the
heresy of Marcellus, as being both dangerous and harmful, and
foreign to the true faith'.[55] In *Letter 80*, Basil attempted to sched-
ule a personal meeting with Athanasius, to no avail. In *Letter 82*,
he appealed to Athanasius to send 'a single letter, advising us
what is to be done.'[56]

While these letters were being written and sent to Athanasius, the church at Ancyra was a strong bastion of Marcellians.
They heard of the issue with Basil and Athanasius, and entered
the debate to intercede for Marcellus and Paulinus. Lienhard
stated, 'A deacon of the group, Eugenius, wrote an exposition
of their faith and carried it to Athanasius in Alexandria. The
Expositio shows that Marcellus was in communion with at least
some bishops in Greece and Macedonia.'[57] The end result of
this action was that Athanasius, along with a synod of bishops in
Alexandria, signed the document which had the opposite effect

---

53. Basil, *Letter 66*, (*NPNF* 2nd series, vol. 8), p. 164.

54. Basil, *Letter 67*, (*NPNF* 2nd series, vol. 8), p. 164.

55. Basil, *Letter 69*, translated by Roy J Deferrari, p. 45.

56. Basil, *Letter 82*, (*NPNF* 2nd series, vol. 8), p. 173.

57. Lienhard, *Contra Marcellum*, p. 8-9.

that Basil had worked to accomplish. When Athanasius signed the document of faith, it meant that Marcellus was accepted by the west. In 372, *Letter 89*, Basil complained to Meletius that 'regarding the most reverend bishop Athanasius, we must remind your perfect wisdom, which knows all accurately, that it is impossible to promote or accomplish any of those things which are necessary by means of letters from me ...'[58]

Interestingly, by this time Basil had notoriety and reputation. Yet the bishops of Alexandria, along with the beloved Athanasius, stood up to him by remaining silent. Athanasius never answered one letter, thus securing the failure of Basil's plan.

Prosopa, ousia and *hypostasis* phase

When his plan to unite the eastern and western church did not materialize, Basil began to write and preach against the heresy of Sabellianism. In the year 373, Basil defined the term *hypostasis* in *Letter 125* in reaction to the Sabellian/Marcellian usage. In the letter, he understood that the Sabellians, particularly his old friend Eustathius of Sebaste, endorsed the Creed of Nicaea. However, Basil, knowing their ploy, stated:

Sabellianism: Sabellianism is named after the third-century monk who propagated the heresy of modalism. The heresy of Sabellianism is that God exists as One but has three different modes of existence at different times. Thus God is one essence and one person. Therefore, the names of Father, Son, and Holy Spirit do not illustrate relationships within the Trinity as there is no trinity. The name Father is used when God's greatness and goodness are considered. The term Son is employed as His revelation to humanity, whereas, Holy Spirit is used when God relates to humanity via His creation, grace, and providence.

It is therefore desirable to receive them with the confession not only that they believe in the words put forth by our fathers at Nicæa, but also according to the sound meaning expressed by those words. For there are men who even in this creed pervert the word of truth, and wrest the meaning of

---

58. Basil, *Letter 89*, translated by Roy J. Deferrari, p. 120.

the words in it to suit their own notions. So Marcellus, when expressing impious sentiments concerning the hypostasis of our Lord Jesus Christ, and describing Him as being Logos and nothing more, had the hardihood to profess to find a pretext for his principles in that creed by affixing an improper sense upon the Homoousion.[59]

Furthermore, Basil indicted Sabellius when he stated:

Some, moreover, of the impious following of the Libyan Sabellius, who understand hypostasis and substance to be identical, derive ground for the establishment of their blasphemy from the same source, because of its having been written in the creed if any one says that the Son is of a different substance or hypostasis, the Catholic and Apostolic Church anathematizes him. But they did not there state hypostasis and substance to be identical. Had the words expressed one and the same meaning, what need of both? It is on the contrary clear that while by some it was denied that the Son was of the same substance with the Father, and some asserted that He was not of the substance and was of some other hypostasis, they thus condemned both opinions as outside that held by the Church.[60]

Basil declared that their misunderstanding of *homoousios* and *ousia* led them to support the creed on wrong terms. In juxtaposition to the Sabellians, Basil comprehended the Father and Son were *homoousios* (a derivative of *ousia*) but that each has their own *hypostasis* (personhood).

The occasion of the letter was to allow Eustathius of Sebaste the opportunity to sign a statement of faith which would clear him of the charges of Arianism. However, the significance of the letter was noted by Lucian Turcescu. He stated, 'Ep. 125 is paramount for Basil's own confession of faith, because it shows his increasing attachment to the Nicene Creed. The entire second section of this letter is occupied by the text of the Nicene creed.'[61]

---

59.   Basil, *Letter 125*, (NPNF 2nd series, vol. 8), p. 194.

60.   Basil, *Letter* p. 125, p. 194.

61.   Lucian Turcescu, 'Prosopon and Hypostasis in Basil of Caesarea's "Against Eunomius" and the Epistles,' *Vigiliae Christianae*, p. 383.

The third section of the letter deals with the divinity of the Holy Spirit. Basil declared that the Holy Spirit is 'holy by nature,'[62] which is to say that He is the same substance or *ousia* as the Father and Son. In this section, Basil began to distinguish the individual hypostasis of each member. He stated that the Father is 'the one Unbegotten,' the Son is 'the Only-begotten,' whereas the Holy Spirit 'proceeds from the Father, and we confess Him to be God without creation.'[63]

Basil developed the defining characteristics of the *hypostasis* of the Trinity along with the issue of one *ousia* or substance. The problem still existed in defining the difference between *hypostasis* and *prosopa* (see below). In Basil's terminology of *prosopa*, the question remains as to the meaning of *hypostasis* with *prosopa* (i.e., synonyms or antonyms).

Letter 214

Basil turned his attention to Antioch once again with *Letter 214*. This letter was written in 375 in order to address the continuing problem of the Arians at Antioch as they had accused Paulinus of Sabellianism. This charge meant that there was no difference between the Father and Son. Concerning this letter, Hildebrand stated, 'In Basil's mind, how the Paulinians related hypostasis and prosopon will determine whether or not they clear themselves of the "Arian" accusation that they are Sabellians.'[64]

The issue at hand was how to define *hypostasis* so that the charge of Sabellianism could be dismantled. In the letter, Basil stated:

> If you ask me to state shortly my own view, I shall state that *ousia* has the same relation to *hypostasis* as the common has to the particular. Every one of us both shares in existence by the common term of *essence* (*ousia*) and by his own properties is such an one

62. Basil, *Letter 125*, (*NPNF* 2nd series, vol. 8), p. 194.

63. Basil, *Letter 125*, p. 195.

64. Hildebrand, *The Trinitarian Theology of Basil of Caesarea*, p. 87.

and such an one. In the same manner, in the matter in question, the term *ousia* is common, like goodness, or Godhead, or any similar attribute; while *hypostasis* is contemplated in the special property of Fatherhood, Sonship, or the power to sanctify.[65]

Basil demonstrated that the *hypostasis* is the property that belongs to the individual member of the Trinity, whereas, *ousia* is what the members share in common to one another. As Hildebrand depicted, Basil distinguished *hypostasis* from *ousia* so that 'it frees *prosopon* of Sabellian connotations.'[66] Thus, the word *hypostasis* becomes a synonym with the word *prosopa*. Therefore, through the efforts of Basil, the Trinitarian formula became known as one *ousia*, three *hypostasis/prosopa*; or one essence, three *prosopa*; or One God, Three Persons!

Against Sabellius, the Arians, and the Anomoeans

The year is 378 and Basil's first homily against the Sabellians[67] is entitled, *Against Sabellius, the Arians, and the Anomoeans.*[68] In this work, Basil refers to Marcellus as a Sabellian. The beginning of the work is pointed as Basil stated that the Sabellians deny 'God from God.'[69] The point is that the Sabellians (actually Marcellus) might confess the Word but their concept does not allow the Word's real existence. Their terminology is that the Father and Son are one *prosopa*. Thus, there is no eternal distinction between Father and Son. Basil argued that the *prosopa* expresses divine plurality. Hildebrand stated, 'Basil promotes *prosopon* in

---

65. Basil, *Letter 214*, (*NPNF* 2nd series, vol. 8), p. 254.

66. Hildebrand, *The Trinitarian Theology of Basil of Caesarea*, p. 87.

67. See chapter 1, footnote 17, p. 26.

68. The actual title is *Contra Sabellianos et Arium et Anomoeos*. See *Patrologiae Cursus Completus* by J. P. Migne, Bernard De Montfaucon's version, 1855. This work contains select documents of the Church Fathers in Latin and Greek. The date of this work is disputed. Hildebrand thinks the work was dated in 372, whereas Fedwick dates the work during the year 378.

69. Basil used most of a work entitled *Ps-Athanasius. Contra Sabellianos. Patrologia Graeca*, pp. 28, 96-121 contains this work. Most scholars denounce this work as not authentic to Athanasius. However, Basil was quite familiar with the work and he used the phrase 'deny God from God' in application to the Sabellians.

this role in polemic reaction to the teachings of Marcellus.'[70] As seen when applied to the Trinity, the word *prosopa* actually means three persons.

Not only did he qualify the meaning between *hypostasis* and *ousia*, but he had to contend with the meaning of *ousia*. For clarification pur-poses, it is worthy of mention that during the writing of *Against Eunomius* Basil took the position that *hypostasis* and *ousia* were basically the same in meaning, or synonyms. Thus, at this point in his life, the theological acumen of Basil was developing rapidly. As a result, Basil began to refine the meaning of the words as a means to confront heresy but also to define orthodox Christianity. Hildebrand gave insight into the rationale of Basil as he had to determine more specific meanings for the words. Hildebrand stated:

Anomoeans: These were also known as the heteroousians. They adhered to the fact that Son was not like the Father in substance. Two well-known members of this group were Aetius and Eunomius. This group was radical in its views while the milder Arians (the homoiousians) were opposed to this position.

A confession of three *prosopa*, however, was not sufficient to guard against the error of Sabellianism; Basil found it necessary to distinguish *hypostasis* from *ousia* ... Basil distinguishes *ousia* from *hypostasis* ... in reaction to the thought of Marcellus of Ancyra and Paulinus of Antioch. More precisely, the distinction of *hypostasis* from *ousia* prevents one from falling into the errors of Marcellus and Sabellius by securing an unconfused understanding of divine plurality and divine unity.[71]

The issue for Basil was that the same words also were used by the Sabellians and Paulinus, which led to the confusion regarding the terminology. In other words, even though they were using the same

---

70. Hildebrand, *The Trinitarian Theology of Basil of Caesarea*, p. 84.

71. Ibid.

language they defined the words differently. Incumbent upon Basil was to make clear distinctions of meaning for each word, which he did, as seen in *Letter 214*.[72]

Because of the confusing definition of *hypostasis* (as understood by the Sabellians), Basil only used the word *prosopa* in *Against Sabellius, the Arians, and the Anomoeans*. In *Against Sabellius*, Lienhard stated that Basil's

> ... terms are more precise. The phrase two *prosopa*, one *ousia* is almost formulaic...He likes to use words for the identity or absolute equality of Father and Son, which is understandable enough in light of the Anomoean opposition ... Basil sees the importance of giving all the titles of the Preincarnate equal weight and not elevating only one as univocal, which was Marcellus' error.[73]

Basil utilized the Trinitarian formula as a means to measure the orthodox Christian faith. Boris Bobrinskoy affirmed the great theological contribution of Basil as he wrote, 'The distinction between the essence and the hypostasis worked out by St. Basil constitutes from then on a definitive asset for Orthodox Trinitarian doctrine, an asset which his companions in arms would faithfully take over.'[74]

2. Public pastoral ministry

Basil's ministry, as a sole Bishop of Caesarea, began in 370. He was elected to replace Eusebius upon his death. However, his official public ministry actually began in 365 as Eusebius recalled Basil to work

---

72. Part of the problem was the language barrier between the Greek east and the Latin west. The words were not easily defined in each language. This led to the doctrinal problem of the Filioque clause. For a historical review of the Filioque problem see, A. Edward Siecienski, *The Filioque: History of a Doctrinal Controversy* (Oxford: Oxford University Press, 2010).

73. Lienhard, *Contra Marcellum*, pp. 230-1.

74. Boris Bobrinskoy, *The Mystery of the Trinity: Trinitarian Experience and Vision in the Biblical and Patristic Tradition* (Crestwood, NY: St. Vladimir's Seminary Press, 1999), p. 234.

with him in the capacity of an associate minister. The reason Basil left Caesarea in 363-4 was because of his difference with Eusebius. Scholars are divided over the exact cause of the split. Charles A. Frazee presented the position that the division of the two men happened over the growing following of Basil's Ascetic/Monastic movement. Frazee stated, 'The number of people devoted to Basil and his ascetic brotherhood grew so large that Bishop Eusebius found the situation unsettling. Basil was sensitive to the problem, and so he retired from active service in Caesarea lest he prove an embarrassment to Eusebius.'[75]

Rousseau had a different perspective on Basil's departure. He recorded Basil's departure in 363-4 as 'a time of turbulence.'[76] The turbulence that Rousseau spoke of was doctrinal division and not just Basil's growing ascetic movement. Referring to the division, Rousseau, paraphrasing Gregory of Nazianzus, suggested that 'some at least thought Eusebius' position to have been uncanonical, if not slightly unorthodox.'[77] The possibility exists that, although Basil received his ordination from Eusebius (362), the two men did not agree on the doctrinal specifics. Furthermore, Basil, being the subordinate, decided to depart rather than cause division in the church. Regardless of the specific reason, Basil left Caesarea in order to prevent further division that would overflow into the church. He honored the pastor, Eusebius, by not being a continual source of contention, thereby showing great respect for the Lord's church and the Lord's pastor at Caesarea.

The political climate at Caesarea began to change with the quest of Valens to adopt Arianism as the official position of the church. Gregory of Nazianzus, sensing the struggle with the

75. Charles A. Frazee, 'Anatolian Asceticism in the Fourth Century: Eustathios of Sebastea and Basil of Caesarea,' *The Catholic Historical Review* 66:1 (Jan. 1980), p. 26.

76. Rousseau, *Basil of Caesarea*, pp. 87-8.

77. Rousseau, *Basil of Caesarea*, p. 134.

Emperor,[78] acknowledged that Eusebius was not as capable to deal with the Emperor as the situation required. He began to write letters to both Eusebius and Basil to secure the return of Basil to Caesarea.[79] Eusebius' decision to recall Basil to Caesarea in 365 was predicated upon the very real threat of heresy. Thus, Basil became a theological aid to Eusebius.

Basil returned to Caesarea to aid Eusebius with the Arian threat. Fedwick, writing about this event, stated, 'From the moment when in 365, with a visit of Valens imminent, Eusebius recalls him to Caesarea, Basil will be seen as uncompromisingly committed to the project of church reform on the pattern of the pre-Constantinian model or, better yet, of the apostolic community of Jerusalem.'[80]

Fortunately for Cappadocia, other political matters intervened as Valens had to deal with the rebellion of the Goths and their leader, Procopius. This uprising kept Valens occupied and, consequently, the imminent threat to Cappadocia subsided for a period of five years.

The famine of Cappadocia

The year 369 proved to be a difficult one for Cappadocia. Caesarea was affected by the drought and subsequent famine in the country. Paul Schroeder described the conditions when he stated, 'Rivers and springs dried up and crops failed, resulting in an acute food shortage

---

78. Gerald R. Reilly, *Imperium and Sacerdotium According to St. Basil the Great* (Washington, D.C.: The Catholic University of America Press, 1945), p. 49. As stated, just one year later, 'Basil and the orthodox believers of the East received confirmation of the Arian tendencies of Valens, when in 366 he called a synod at Nicodemia with the intention of bringing Arianism into power.'

79. See Gregory's *Letters 16-18* sent to Eusebius as *Letters 8, 19* to Basil.

80. Fedwick, *The Church and the Charisma of Leadership in Basil of Caesarea*, p. 14. According to Gregory of Nazianzus, Valens did visit and subjected Eusebius to debate with the Homoeans. Eusebius performed poorly which prompted him, at the encouragement of Gregory, to recall Basil. See Gregory's letters as mentioned in footnote 79.

throughout the region.'[81] In response to this, Basil began to imple-
ment a Christian social order. However, this social order was not designed to restructure society. Rather, the goal was to alleviate the suf-
fering and poverty of the church and the surrounding community.

The very purpose of the new order consisted in the establishment of the *Ptochotrophium* or Poor House.[82] Gregory of Nazianzen, in his tribute to Basil, stated, 'For by his word and advice he
opened the stores of those who possess them, and so, according
to Scripture dealt food to the hungry, and satisfied the poor with
bread, and fed them in the time of dearth, and filled the hungry
souls with good things.'[83] The 'good things' Gregory referred to
is the ministry of Word to accompany the ministry of the deed
(as seen). Demetrios Constantelos accurately observed:

> For Basil, to love God meant to love man, whatever man's physi-
> cal condition or background ... His great concern for the needy,
> the sick, the suffering, and the forgotten received its inspiration
> from what John the Evangelist wrote: 'he who does not love his
> brother whom he has seen, he cannot love God whom he has
> not seen.' For Basil, doctrine and canon, worship and ethics,
> word and behavior were inextricably woven.[84]

Ministry of the Word

Basil's legacy as a pastor/preacher is remarkable in that the
modern pastor has an example of a pastor who modified the
church's worship practice based upon the content of Scripture.
The issue of worship for Basil was born out of the communication
of the Scriptures as they revealed the holiness of God. Hugh

---

81. C. Paul Schroeder, *Introduction to On Social Justice* (Crestwood, NY: St. Vladimir's
     Seminary Press, 2009), p. 21.

82. Fedwick, *The Charisma of Church Leadership,* p. 38. *Patrologia Graeca* 36 also terms
     this the *Basiliad* or *Basil's New City.*

83. Gregory of Nazianzen, *The Panegyric on St. Basil,* (*NPNF* 2nd series, vol. 7), p. 407.

84. Demetrios J. Constantelos, 'Basil the Great's Social Thought and Involvement,'
     The Greek Orthodox Theological Review 2:1-2 (March 1, 1981), p. 82.

Thomson Kerr, enamored with Basil's preaching, described his sermons as bearing 'the stamp of a man of passionate eloquence and moral courage.'[85]

Worship

The background of the revision of the liturgy was the Arian theology.[86] The Arians basically denied the divinity of Christ and the second phase of Arianism denied the divinity of the Holy Spirit. In response to the defective Arian theology, Basil utilized a different version of the doxology as he prayed with his congregation. He depicted this in his famous work, *On the Holy Spirit.* Basil stated:

> Lately while I pray with the people, we sometimes finish the doxology to God the Father with the form, 'Glory to the Father *with* the Son, *together* with the Holy Spirit,' and at other times we use 'Glory to the Father, through the Son in the Holy Spirit.' Some of those present accused us of using strange and mutually contradictory terms. But your wish certainly is to help these people, or, if they should prove completely incurable, to safeguard those who associate with them ...[87]

The theological content of the new liturgy addressed the worship of the people. Basil desired that the congregation acknowledge the deity of the Holy Spirit. Haykin stated, 'Moreover, as the church baptizes, so must she teach and so must she worship. If she baptizes in the name of the Father and of the Son and of the Holy Spirit, she must teach the deity of the three and the propriety of their worship.'[88] Basil's liturgy is used still by the Greek Orthodox Church. Such is the impact of teaching the church to worship in a form that is based upon the Scriptures.

---

85. Hugh Thomson Kerr, *Preaching in the Early Church* (New York, NY: Fleming H. Revell Company, 1942), p. 166.

86. See Chapter One for an overview of the Arian crisis.

87. Basil, *On the Holy Spirit,* pp. 17-18.

88. Haykin, *Rediscovering the Church Fathers,* p. 122.

Liturgy: The Greek word is *leitourgia* and has the meaning of service or ministry. The New Testament uses this word to describe services used in worship. Later in patristic thought, the liturgy began to have a technical usage as a standard of practice for worship services especially in regard to the Lord's Supper. However, the New Testament does not establish particular forms for worship. Nonetheless, the practice became so very widespread that it allowed the technical usage to have prominence in the forms of worship throughout Christianity.

Preaching

Basil systematically preached the whole counsel of God. Perhaps one of his greatest accomplishments was the series on Genesis entitled, *On the Hexaemeron*.[89] These nine sermons were delivered during the Lenten week in 378. His approach to Genesis still speaks to the modern Evangelical pastor as Basil interpreted Genesis to be literal concerning creation.[90] Basil's interpretation, then and now, is considered to be in opposition to the allegorical method that was so common in the ancient Christian world.[91] His preaching on these topics demonstrated the need for the congregation to understand the world's order, humanity's existence within the world, and humanity's creation in the image of God. The legacy of this sermon series is that Basil presented a complete cosmology that is foundational for the modern world.

Basil's preaching consisted of theological, as well as, practical application. He did not separate the theological from the practical but understood that theology was practical. This is demonstrated in his sermons that dealt with the poverty and famine of Caesarea.

---

89. Saint Basil, *Exegetical Homilies*, trans., Agnes Clare Way, *Fathers of the Church* 46 (Washington, D.C.: Catholic University of America Press, 1963).

90. A chapter will be dedicated to the *Hexaemeron*; therefore, the discussion at this point will be brief.

91. Richard Lim, 'The Politics of Interpretation in Basil of Caesarea's Hexaemeron,' *Vigiliae Christianae* 44 (1990), p. 351.

In his sermon, *I Will Tear Down My Barns*,[92] Basil preached the text from Luke 12:16–21. He preached against the stinginess of the people who would not share their food with those who were hungry. In that sermon, Basil stated that the wealthy could have imitated Joseph but instead they 'rob others of benefit.'[93]

Although Basil was practical in his preaching, he did not neglect the sole purpose of preaching (i.e., the gospel message). Fedwick stated, 'According to Basil, the preacher, through his work of preparing souls to surrender to the will of Christ, heals the wounds occasioned by sin and restores them to the life of divine grace.'[94] Thus, his preaching focused upon the gospel proclamation.

Basil's preaching also demonstrated his love for the church as a whole. In Homily 17 on the Psalms (sermon on Psalm 44) he underscored the priority of the church's discernment of the presence of God in the world. Basil stated, 'He summons the Church to hear and observe the precepts ... He teaches that she has a mind trained to contemplation through the word.'[95] Thus, his passion for the pulpit included the spiritual development of the body of Christ.

Continuing Theological Development

During the years 374 and 375, Basil made what could be considered his most lasting contribution to theology with the publication of *On the Holy Spirit*.[96] The basic thesis is that the Holy Spirit is divine and should be reverenced as such. Basil also developed the concept that without the Spirit there is no contemplation of the Word. Therefore, the Arians who fight the Spirit cannot

---

92. A modern translation of this sermon is found in C. Paul Schroeder's *On Social Justice* (Crestwood, NY: St. Vladimir's Seminary Press, 2009). For clarification of Schroeder's work, he retitled Basil's Homily 6 with the new title of '*I Will Tear Down My Barns*.'

93. Basil, *I Will Tear Down My Barns*, trans., C. Paul Schroeder, *On Social Justice* (Crestwood, NY: St. Vladimir's Seminary Press, 2009), p. 62.

94. Fedwick, *The Church and the Charisma of Leadership*, p. 166.

95. Saint Basil, *Homily 17 on the Psalms*, trans., Agnes Clare Way, *Fathers of the Church* 46 (Washington, DC: Catholic University of America Press, 1963), pp. 291-2.

96. A chapter will be devoted to this work, so the comments in this chapter will be brief.

know Christ since, in their defective theology, the Holy Spirit is not God. Basil depicted the fact that the Spirit is to 'confess the true identity of Christ' and thus allowing a proper form of worship of the true God.[97]Bobrinskoy stated that Basil helped to 'clarify this initiatory and illuminating role of the Spirit that makes the vision of God possible.'[98]

Reward in heaven

Basil did not have a healthy body as he was ill most of the time and prone to sickness all of the time. He died at the young age of 50, on 1 January 379. His legacy is monumental as his theology won the day for the orthodox party at the second ecumenical council (i.e., the Council of Constantinople in 381).

Basil demonstrated that the institutional church cannot be united to a government that seeks to destroy the biblical position. The union of church and state was ripped apart in the eastern portion of the Empire. When Valens supported the Council of Rimini, at the time Julian received baptism by an Arian bishop, and as priests and bishops were capitulating to the Emperor, Basil stood for the Lord by proclaiming and defending the orthodox doctrine of the Trinity.

Basil's contribution to Evangelicalism

Basil has given the church a strong legacy in which the modern Evangelical pastor or preacher can appreciate.

The Scriptures

Basil's sermons were delivered to the congregation with the understanding that the preacher was God's appointed herald of truth. His exegesis of the text took the literal position so that the simple understanding of God was revealed clearly in each

---

97. Basil, *On the Holy Spirit*, pp. 66 and 74.

98. Boris Bobrinskoy, 'The Indwelling of the Spirit of Christ: "Pneumatic Christology" in the Cappadocian Fathers,' *St. Vladimir's Theological Quarterly* 28:1 (January 1, 1984), p. 56.

sermon. Basil did build upon the issue of tradition but that did not hinder him from accepting the truthfulness and veracity of each Scriptural text.

His sermons were Christ-centered. The homilies depicted a systematic theologian striving to proclaim the truth of Christ from the Old Testament and the New Testament. His concept of spirituality developed the body of believers, centered upon the Holy Spirit revealing the truth of Christ to the congregant. Thus, his harshness towards the Arians is simply not a vendetta. On the contrary, Basil knew that truth must be proclaimed to the church through the power of the Holy Spirit revealing the mysteries of Christ.

The church

Basil understood that there is one true church that proclaims the message of Christ to the people. The church cannot compromise with the imperial authorities although it certainly can cooperate with civil magistrates. The areas in which Basil should be an example to modern Evangelicals are twofold. First, there is worship and the church. Basil often is accused of implementing a novel approach to worship. However, the context of his innovation must be examined closely. The Arians reinterpreted the liturgy of the church to proclaim the sole monarchy of the Father. This was not the intention but after decades of controversy the clarity of the liturgy was confused. Basil instituted a form of worship through a different liturgical formula in order to clarify the meaning of the Trinity. Therefore, what was proclaimed in the pulpit also was worshiped by the congregation. He did not contemporize (or innovate) a style of worship to reach a contemporary audience (as is often done today). He innovated to bring the truth of God's Word to the people of God so that the doxology was theologically orthodox. In other words, the worship of the church was supported and even imbedded with the truth of God.

Second, there is social ministries and the church. The church engaged in social ministries, as seen in the *Ptochotrophium* or Poor House. Basil's pastoral ministry was not simply a spiritual approach at the neglect of the needs of the people. He led his bishopric to address the social concerns of the people as an opportunity to impact them with the gospel. Again, this is evidence that Basil interpreted the Scriptures literally as the Old Testament patriarch, Joseph, was his model for sharing community goods with the city of Caesarea.

Theological development

Basil continued to strive to understand the nature of God. His work and studies revealed that his journey to orthodoxy went through various phases. However, that is not a negative issue for the pastor or preacher. That fact reveals a man who struggles to know the heart and mind of God. His struggle to define terms that were precise in communication is an example for Evangelicals to take the calling of God seriously so that the very words the modern preacher utilizes will be reflective of God's nature.

His theological legacy has been relegated to a historical footnote in the last generation. However, Basil's Trinitarian truth (or formula) of God must be reclaimed by the current Evangelical pastor. The church desperately needs men who have theological acumen as they develop sermons, engage in ministry, and lead the church to worship the one God revealed in three persons. May this present generation recover that practical, spiritual, and theological legacy of St. Basil.

3

SOLACE IN THE DESERT

Asceticism via monasticism was introduced in the last chapter as a way to address the morally bankrupt church of the fourth century. However, monasticism as a spiritual movement has a history prior to the fourth century. William Harmless acknowledged Egypt as the traditional starting place for monasticism. However, he does admit that the Egyptian theory is only 'partially true.'[1] Harmless came to the conclusion that the origin of monasticism was a 'messy diverse phenomenon.'[2]

> **Monasticism:** The monastic was a monk or nun who lived in isolation. The beginning of monasticism started with the idea of a life of commitment modeled in the Old Testament (Elijah) and the New Testament (John the Baptist). This lifestyle involves the renunciation of personal property, chastity, and the embracing of poverty, prayer, reading, and work. This facilitates the ability to achieve the goal of dedication to the Lord by means of purity of heart and body.

The indication is that there are many origins of monasticism. The movements appeared to be sporadic but independent of

1. William Harmless, *Desert Christians: An Introduction to the Literature of Early Monasticism* (Oxford, England: Oxford University Press, 2004), p. 17.

2. Ibid., p. 448.

each other. As a result, monasticism does not have a direct lineage. Therefore, it is hard to conclude who was identified as the first monastic.

Saint Anthony, the Anchoritic monk

The traditional Christian model began with St. Anthony. In fact, Augustine Holmes stated that monasticism began with 'St. Anthony in Egypt and from there spread throughout the Christian world during the fourth century.'[3] The fact that Athanasius wrote a biography on St. Anthony reveals the depth of the latter's influence.[4]

Anchoritic monasticism: This form of monasticism is the total withdrawal of the individual from society. It is the earliest form of the monastic endeavor. The word 'hermit' is often associated with the concept of this form of monasticism. The lifestyle is one of prayer, it is focused on the Eucharist, and strives to attain an ascetic manner.

St. Anthony died in A.D. 356 after a long and prosperous life (the dating of Anthony's life is from the years 251 to 356). Anthony's time in history placed him in the time frame of the Arian controversy which was rampant throughout Christianity. Seemingly, it is no secret that Athanasius gave the impression that Anthony detested the Arian doctrine.[5] Harmless stated that Athanasius' biography on Anthony is little more than 'political propaganda.'[6]

---

3. Augustine Holmes, *The Spirituality of the Rules of St. Basil* (Kalamazoo, MI: Cistercian Publications, 2000), p. 26.

4. Athanasius, *The Life of Anthony*, trans. Robert Gregg, *The Classics of Western Spirituality* (New York, NY: Paulist Press, 1980). This translation is readable and easy to acquire.

5. Ibid., see chapters 68–70, 89, and 91. Conceivably, Athanasius used his work on Anthony as a mouthpiece to denounce Arianism. Thus, parts of the story may be more fictional than biographical. However, the Arian doctrine was known widely, therefore, it is possible that Anthony did know of Arianism and reject its influence. The church at Alexandria had imbibed with this heretical teaching and that fact may have been a motive for desert withdrawal. The truth of the issue is difficult to ascertain.

6. Harmless, *Desert Christians*, p. 93.

Regardless of the motive, Anthony gave the impression that he embraced the life of a hermit as a positive response to asceticism as a means of pleasing God. Thus, through devotion to God, in isolation, he followed the example of Christ in the temptation narratives, and learned obedience in order to live godly. Anthony became the popular, model hermit/monk of anchoritic monasticism.

Pachomius, the Coenobitic monk

Pachomius lived during the years 290–346. He was born in upper Egypt, converted to Christianity after his discharge from the military, and founded a monastery at Tabennisi.[7] The monastery grew so large that by the end of Pachomius' life he was the abbot over nine monasteries, which included two for women. He was one of the first to organize monasticism into communal living. Pachomius lived his life in relation to other monks, which is known as coenobitic or communal living. This movement was in contrast to the anchoritic approach.

> **Coenobitic monasticism:** This form of monasticism is an organized community where the adherents live in small rooms or huts and form a monastery. They are community-based, often working together for the common good of the monastery. The monks understand that asceticism is the primary goal to achieve the holiness of the Lord in community with one another.

Pachomius was a mastermind. When he founded the monastery at Tabennisi, he began to train the monks in a communal lifestyle. His concept was to formulate rules that demanded strict adherence to ensure that monks were practicing holiness in relation to one another. The means to ensure commitment to the monastic lifestyle became known as the Rules of Pachomius.[8]

7. F. L. Cross and E. A. Livingstone, *The Oxford Dictionary of the Christian Church*, 3rd ed. (Oxford: Oxford University Press, 1997), s.v. 'Pachomius, St.'

8. Philip Schaff, *Nicene and Post-Nicene Christianity: From Constantine the Great to Gregory the Great A.D. 311-590*, vol. 3 of *History of the Christian Church* (Peabody, MA: Hendrickson Publishers, 2006), p. 196.

These rules served to govern the life of the monks as they related to each other in the cloister.

The spread of Pachomius' version of monasticism was accomplished as his influence moved east. Philip Schaff stated, 'From Egypt the cloister life spread with the rapidity of the irresistible spirit of the age, over the entire Christian East. The most eminent fathers of the Greek church were either themselves monks for a time, or at all events friends and patrons of monasticism.'[9]

Monastic trip

Shortly after his salvation, Basil toured the monasteries of Egypt, Palestine, Syria, and Mesopotamia.[10] Basil traveled through various countries during the majority of the year 356. This trip to the eastern monasteries may have helped shape Basil's understanding of monasticism. He stated in his *Letter 223* that it was during this trip he studied the lifestyle of the ascetic monks:

> I admired their continence in living, and their persistency in prayer, and at their triumphing over sleep; subdued by no natural necessity, ever keeping their souls' purpose high and free, in hunger, in thirst, in cold, in nakedness, they never yielded to the body; they were never willing to waste attention on it; always, as though living in a flesh that was not theirs, they showed in very deed what it is to sojourn for a while in this life, and what to have one's citizenship and home in heaven.[11]

Basil was impressed with the commitment displayed by the monks. His return to Pontus provided him with the opportunity to contemplate asceticism via monasticism. Basil wanted to 'interweave the moral with the social and practical aspects of Christianity.'[12]

Returning home in early 357, Basil went to Pontus to the family estate at Annesi to practice communal asceticism with his fam-

---

9.   Schaff, *Nicene and Post-Nicene Christianity: From Constantine the Great to Gregory the Great A.D. 311-590*, p. 198.

10. Basil, '*Letter 223*,' (*NPNF* 2:8), p. 263.

11. Ibid.

12. Rousseau, *Basil of Caesarea*, p. 190.

ily. At this time, his mother, sister, and entire household were living at the estate in a family communal arrangement. Finally, he retreated to the Iris River to begin a coenobitic monastic movement. He remained in that environment from 358 to 364.

Monastic reform

Although Basil admired the monks' lifestyle, there were certain problems with the ascetic approach. He recognized that the structure was more legalistic than spiritual. While Basil did not reject the monasticism of the Egyptians and Syrians entirely, his conception of asceticism allowed more of a communal environment rather than one that isolated the individual from community. As Michael Haykin stated, 'Basil, on the other hand, would be a pioneer of coenobitic monasticism – a monasticism centered on living the Christian life together with others who were like-minded.'[13] The rationale for this new form of asceticism was that he had witnessed some of the glaring problems with asceticism in his previous travels. In no fewer than four letters, he addressed those problems. Margaret Murphy stated:

> He composes four letters bearing directly on these problems. Three of these, Ep. II (Letter 2), XIV (14), and XXII (22) were written between the establishment of the monastery at Pontus and the beginning of the composition of the *Ascetica* and should obviously be scrutinized for similarities or differences from the *Ascetica* themselves. The fourth, EP. CCXXIII (223), while written long years after the *Ascetica* were begun (375), treats of the very beginning of his ascetical life.[14]

The fact that Basil contemplated a reform movement within monasticism reveals that he did not consider the movement without merit. However, he understood that monasticism needed reform in some of its deficiencies.

---

13. Haykin, *Rediscovering the Church Fathers*, p. 109.

14. Margaret Murphy, *St. Basil and Monasticism* (New York, NY: AMS Press, 1971), p. 13.

Doctrinal, as well as behavioral problems existed among the monastics. Basil observed monks who often were in rebellion against local priests and even bishops. He addressed authority when he composed the rules for monastic life but did so in a biblical manner. Rousseau wrote, 'He was cautious in describing the honor due to them; it was to be enjoyed in a context of mutual humility, which would oblige superiors as much as their subjects.'[15] Basil did not seek to discredit leadership but his desire was to guard against pride. According to Basil, the proper authority for the Christian monastic, as well as all Christians, was Jesus Christ as revealed in the Scriptures. As Margaret Murphy wrote, 'The very first body of regulations drawn up for his monks was taken entirely from Scripture.'[16] Basil's writings focused upon the Scriptures and are rooted deeply in the gospel message. Thus, any reform for monasticism would seem to be a reform for the entire church.

The rationale for coenobitic reform

One of the basic problems with early monasticism was the tendency to focus on one's personal achievements, which led to pride. According to Haykin, monasticism had a 'tendency toward spiritual elitism and egoism, and its failure to cultivate a spirit of humility and love for one's neighbor. Partly this was due to the fact that Egyptian and Syrian monasticism was eremitic in orientation, which led to isolationism and the tendency to be focused on one's achievements.'[17] Basil perceived that the Christian life should be lived in and through ecclesial relationships. William Kemp Lowther Clarke summarized Basil's *Rule* 7 to demonstrate that Basil had a corporate view of the Christian life in mind. Clarke stated:

1. We are none of us self-sufficient in the matter of providing for our bodily needs.

---

15. Rousseau, *Basil of Caesarea*, p. 221.

16. Margaret Murphy, *St. Basil and Monasticism*, p. 41.

17. Haykin, *Rediscovering the Church Fathers*, p. 109.

2. Solitude is antagonistic to the law of love, since the solitary is bound to serve his own interests.

3. It is harmful to the soul, when we have no one to rebuke us for our faults.

4. Certain specific Christian duties, such as feeding the hungry and clothing the naked, are impossible for the true solitary.

5. We are all members one of another and Christ is our Head. If we separate from our brethren, how can we keep our relation to Christ intact?

6. We have different spiritual gifts. The solitary buries his one gift, but in a coenobium each shares in the gifts of the brethren.

7. Most important of all, the solitary is in danger of self-pleasing, and thinking he has already attained perfection. In the nature of things, he cannot practice humility, pity or long-suffering.[18]

Again, Basil seemed to reject the isolationism of the monastic movement simply because his devotion to the Scriptures compelled him to think ecclesiologically.

Gregory of Nazianzen's, *The Panegyeric on St. Basil*, described how Basil combined two concepts to form a different approach to monasticism. The terms *solitary life* and *mixed life* suggested that Basil understood the command to love one another could be accomplished only if there was interaction between the church and the world. Gregory stated that Basil 'united the solitary and the community life.'[19] Clarke gave the translation as 'ascetics living in the world.'[20]

18. William Kemp Lowther Clarke, *Saint Basil the Great: A Study in Monasticism* (Cambridge: Cambridge University Press, 1912), pp. 86-7.

19. Gregory of Nazianzen, *The Panegyric on St. Basil* (*NPNF* 2nd series, vol. 7), p. 415.

20. Clarke, *A Study in Monasticism*, p. 112.

In the new form, the communal life was to live separately from the world but relate to the world so as to have influence upon it. Thus, the monk who served the church was not to live in isolation, but to live and work in such a way that his or her life could have a profound spiritual impact on the church which had compromised itself with worldliness. The key to this influence was genuine Christian love and correct orthodoxy. Basil's approach to monasticism was tied doctrinally to the church as he continued to clarify his own theological position. Yet, the interesting fact must be stated so as not to misinterpret his heart: Basil loved the church and tried to find solutions to the doctrinal problems that existed within the fourth-century church. Demetrios Constantelos commented about Basil's core belief that ministry is essential to the church. He stated that Basil 'believed that the Christian theologian or churchman neglects his true role if theology is pursued in academic, monastic, or ecclesiastical isolation from social existence'.[21] Therefore, the solution was to be separate from the world and engaged with ecclesiastical life.

In order to understand Basil, one must review three works that are related directly to coenobitic living. They are *The Moral Rules*, *The Large Asceticon*, and his sermon, *On Humility*.

The moral rules

The Moral Rules (*Moralia*) were written in approximately 359–60.[22] The work describes the actions of Christians based upon the revelation of the Scriptures. Fedwick stated that this work 'reviews all the different charismata that Christians might possess. The functions surveyed range from those of the leaders of the church ... to the ethos of married people; husbands, wives, children, widows, soldiers, rulers and the order of virgins.'[23]

---

21. Demetrios J. Constantelos, 'Basil the Great's Social Thought and Involvement,' *Greek Orthodox Theological Review* 26:1–2 (March 1, 1981), p. 82.

22. Basil, *Ascetical Works*, tr. Monica Wagner, *Fathers of the Church*, vol. 9 (Washington, D.C: Catholic University of America Press, 1950).

23. Fedwick, *The Church and the Charisma of Leadership in Basil of Caesarea*, p. 98.

This work contains eighty rules that depict how Christians in general and monks in particular are to embrace the call of the Lord and conduct themselves accordingly. Two of the more noteworthy rules that deal with this issue are rule seven and rule eight. Rule seven states, 'That even if a man seem to confess the Lord and hear His words, but does not obey His commands, he is condemned, even though, by some divine concession, he be vouchsafed an endowment of spiritual gifts.'[24] The issue, for Basil, is that obedience to the commands of Christ is evidence of one's calling to ministry.

Rule eight follows the thoughts of one's obedience by relating the calling to serve with the test of faith. What is revealing is that the test of faith is related directly to how one acknowledges the veracity and inerrancy of the Scriptures. This rule states, 'That we must neither doubt nor hesitate respecting the words of the Lord, but be fully persuaded that every word is true and possible even if nature rebel; for therein is the test of faith.'[25]

This rule basically affirms the Evangelical position that inerrancy is the only acceptable theological position that evidences a call to ministry. Thus, according to Basil, obedience is obedience to the authority of the Word of God.

The issue of theological disobedience also is addressed. Rule forty states, 'That they who introduce erroneous doctrines, however subtly, to delude or confound the unstable should not be tolerated.'[26] The concept of biblical and doctrinal fidelity to the Scriptures must be the identifying characteristic of a man who embraces his calling to follow the Lord in ministry. The *Moral Rules* are to aid the monastic specifically and the church generally to engage in holiness. The worldliness of the church only can be dealt with by taking the Scriptures as authoritative for the practice of godly living. Thus, any rejection of the Scriptures

---

24. Fedwick, *The Church and the Charisma of Leadership in Basil of Caesarea*, p. 80.

25. Ibid.

26. Ibid., p. 118.

assures the negative consequences of a church that has compromised with the world and must repent of its own worldliness.

'The Large Asceticon'

During the 360s, Basil founded many new monasteries and reformed numerous others. Haykin observed, 'His *Longer Rules* and *Shorter Rules* were written for the regulation of life in these communities.'[27] Yet these *Rules* constituted a way of life that was reflective of the Scriptures. The *Rules* 'represent a collection of eighty Scripture references in the form of an index, as it were, intended to guide the reader in his or her reading of the Bible'.[28]

Basil's idea of reform had the Bible as its basis for the primary source of spiritual life. Basil understood that the Christian life is one of worship and inherently spiritual by design. Regarding Basil's conception, Metropolitan Georges Khodr wrote, 'Any action undertaken by the Christian should be spiritual by nature. Any thought, word, gesture, or other activity of the body or of the heart should be inspired and guided by the Holy Spirit.'[29] Thus, the Scriptures were to be primary in the life of the believer, and the Holy Spirit would illuminate the Christian as he read them and implemented the teachings in his life. Rousseau concluded that Basil 'emphasized a human awareness of the power and the activity of God and stressed the way in which the very vocabulary of Scripture brought the creature into relationship with God'.[30]

The initial *Rules* were written in approximately 359–60. However, although they served as the basis for reform in his early ministry, Basil revised the final version, entitled *Great Asceticon*.

---

27. Haykin, *Rediscovering the Church Fathers*, p. 111.

28. Hubertus R. Drobner, *The Fathers of the Church: A Comprehensive Introduction*, trans. Siegfried S. Schatzmann (Peabody, MA: Hendrickson Publishers, 2007), p. 359.

29. Metropolitan Georges (Khodr), 'Basil the Great: Bishop and Pastor,' *St. Vladimir's Theological Quarterly* 29 (Jan. 1985), p. 15.

30. Rousseau commented upon Basil's work *Contra Eunomium* (*Against Eunomius*) but the quote is true for Basil's theological conclusions about all of Scripture. Rousseau, *Basil of Caesarea*, p. 128.

The structure of The *Great Asceticon* is 'divided into the Longer Rule, with 55 questions and answers, and the Shorter Rule, with 313; in this case, the terms 'longer' and 'shorter' do not refer to the number of questions answered but to the detailed treatment of the answers.'[31] Basil's *Rules* so shaped monasticism in Cappadocia that, according to Haykin, 'Basilian monasticism became the inspiration for Benedictine monasticism which flourished in Western Europe between 500 and 1000 A.D.'[32]

The content of the rules

One of the more notable rules is found in question two, which asks about humanity's ability to love God and keep the Lord's commandments. Basil established the position that humanity's love for God is a natural inclination. In his reply, Basil utilized a term from Stoic philosophy, *spermatikos tis logos*. Properly translated, the term means 'rational seed.' Holmes reviewed the meaning of the phrase and concluded:

> The term is sometimes used by them [Christian writers] broadly in the Stoic sense without assimilation to Christ the Logos, for example as 'generative principles' in Origen's discussion of the virgin birth ... the term is developed in a Christian direction. Justin in his Second Apology, Chapters 8 and 13, would seem to use the adjective *spermatikos* in an active sense, thus 'the seed-sowing word'. For him the 'seeds of the word' are a sort of immanent revelation of which all men partake and which is perfected in Christianity.[33]

Basil used the term but gave it a different meaning as his 'use of the term is closer to the original idea of a dynamic constitutive principle placed in creatures by the Creator.'[34] The significance of the meaning is that God placed in humanity, at creation, the

---

31. Drobner, *The Fathers of The Church*, p. 360.

32. Haykin, *Rediscovering the Church Fathers*, p. 111.

33. Augustine Holmes, *The Spirituality of the Rules of St. Basil*, p. 72.

34. Ibid., p. 73.

capacity or natural tendency to love God. In other words, the seed was implanted to love. Holmes stated, 'Basil thus follows earlier Fathers, profoundly Christianizes this Hellenistic idea and integrates it into his own scheme based on love and the commandments. It is also not merely an abstract theory but explains an anthropology based on experience: no one taught us to love our parents.'[35] Basil understood that the commandment to love God (Matthew 22:37–40) is issued for all humanity. In order to fulfill that command, the capacity to do so must be innate within humanity's creation. Basil stated, 'Having received, therefore, a command to love God, we have possessed the innate power of loving from the first moment of our creation.'[36]

The issue concerning humanity's love for God is thwarted by the fact that humanity's free will is perverted and no longer can discern what is truly beautiful and desirable. Basil made the point that even though humanity 'fell into sin, and by sin into death and its attendant evils, God did not forsake him [humanity].'[37] Basil described the *Heilsgeschichte* (salvation history of redemption) to demonstrate that humanity was redeemed from sin and once again is capable of responding to God's love. Basil stated, 'Nor was He [God] content with merely bringing back to life those who were dead, but He conferred upon them the dignity of divinity and prepared them for everlasting rest transcending every human concept in the magnitude of its joy.'[38]

Question three correlates to question two which is based upon Matthew 22:37–40. The greatest commandment is to love God and in order to demonstrate that love, humanity must love their neighbors. Basil wrote, 'Who does not know that man is a civilized and gregarious animal, neither savage nor a lover of solitude! Nothing, indeed is so compatible with our nature as

35. Augustine Holmes, *The Spirituality of the Rules of St. Basil*, p. 74.

36. Basil, *Ascetical Works*, p. 234.

37. Ibid., p. 237.

38. Ibid., p. 238.

living in society and in dependence upon one another as loving our own kind.'[39]

The theological concept and specific terms Basil used demonstrated that he rejected solitude as normal. First, the command to love God overflows into a love for one's neighbor. The basic theological premise is that love for God is illustrated by loving one's neighbor. Thus, for Basil, 'It is, accordingly, possible to keep the second commandment by observing the first, and by means of the second, we are led back to the first. He who loves the Lord loves his neighbor.'[40]

The specific term Basil utilized is a biblical term that would not go unnoticed by those who read Greek. The term 'gregarious' is translated from the Greek word *koinonikon*. The form of this word is found in the New Testament, describing the fellowship of the early church. Acts 2:44 uses the word *koiva*, which is a form of *koinonikon*. The basic meaning is that which is 'common.' Basil used the word to describe a communal or common life that must exist within the church. Holmes stated that Basil used this word to 'exhort the ascetics to ... accept the community life *(he epi to auto zoe)* in imitation of the apostolic way of life *(politeia)*.'[41] The meaning is clear (i.e., that isolation is not biblically representative of the Christian life or of the ecclesia).

Although Basil rejected isolation, he encouraged communal living. Adalbert de Vogüé commented that Basil understood 'Love of God and love of neighbor, then, leads to living away from the world, in community.'[42] The concept of communal life meant that the monastic was to withdraw from the world in order to prepare spiritually for ministry. Question seven reveals this issue in his explanation. Basil stated, 'If we are not joined together by union

39. Basil, *Ascetical Works*, p. 239.

40. Ibid., p. 240.

41. Holmes, *The Spirituality of the Rules of St. Basil*, p. 148.

42. Adalbert de Vogüé, 'The Greater Rules of Saint Basil – A Survey,' in *Word and Spirit, A Monastic Review*, ed. S.M. Clare (Still River, MA: St. Bede's Publications, 1979), p. 53.

in the Holy Spirit in the harmony of one body, but each of us should choose to live in solitude, we would not serve the common good in the ministry according to God's good pleasure, but would be satisfying our own passion for self-gratification.'[43] Basil understood the church to be the place where the Holy Spirit ministers through gifts that are bestowed upon the members. Since 'no one has the capacity to receive all the spiritual gifts,' each member, living communally, 'enjoys his own gift and enhances it by giving others a share, besides reaping benefit from the gifts of others as if they were his own.'[44]

The Large Asceticon illustrated Basil's coenobitic approach to monasticism. They revealed Basil's method to enhance the ministry of the church rather than isolate it. As Clarke adequately stated, 'He thus enlisted the services of monasticism to strengthen the Church.'[45] The basic form of his approach is that ministry must be given to others and not isolated from the church or the world.

The sermon, 'Of Humility'

This sermon characterized the ethical and theological mindset of Basil. His life and ministry can be and should be stated in a single word — humility! For Basil, the single most important characteristic of a leader was humility before the Lord and the watching world. This aspect of humility was patterned after the Lord as depicted in Matthew 11:28-29. The word 'lowly' is the Greek word tapeinos. Haykin noted, 'Christ here describes himself as the ultimate embodiment of humility. Henceforth, all who genuinely called him Lord would seek to reproduce in their lives the Master's humility. And when the early Christians reflected on the meaning of Christ's coming into this world, his humility was central to their reflections.'[46]

---

43. Basil, Ascetical Works, p. 249.

44. Ibid., p. 250.

45. Clarke, Saint Basil the Great: A Study in Monasticism, p. 120.

46. Haykin, Rediscovering the Church Fathers, p. 112.

The thought of Christ's humility is central to Basil in that the sermon, *Of Humility*, demonstrated the fact that humanity's restoration cannot be achieved unless humility of soul is present. Basil stated, 'The surest salvation for him [humanity], the remedy of his ills, and the means of restoration of his original state is in practicing humility...'[47] The practice of humility is in opposition to humanity's current state of existence but also contradicts the tactics of Satan against humanity. For Basil, the temptation of Satan to entice humanity was to achieve a 'false glory.'[48]

The root of this false glory lies at the heart of humanity's rebellion against the Lord. The same rebellion is nothing less than following the example of Satan as he attempted to take glory from God and bestow it upon himself. Therefore, Basil warned, 'Take care not to repeat the fall of the Devil. He, in exalting himself above man, fell at the hands of man, and is delivered up to be trodden upon as a footstool to him who had been under his heel.'[49] The warning is that humanity's pride also will be rejected by the Lord.

Basil understood that the issue of pride stands contrary to the disposition of humility. Thus, the question Basil posed is, 'How shall we, casting off the deadly weight of pride, descend to saving humility?'[50] He answered his own question by encouraging humanity's actions to be 'free from pomposity.'[51] One might assume that Basil was advocating a works-based salvation or had elevated good works to legalism. However, that simply is not the case. He wrote, 'Now, this is the perfect and consummate glory in God: not to exult in one's own justice, but, recognizing oneself as lacking true justice, to be justified by faith in Christ alone.'[52] Concerning the claim of legalism, Basil wrote, 'God also reveals

47.   Basil, *Ascetical Works*, p. 475.

48.   Ibid.

49.   Ibid., p. 482.

50.   Ibid., p. 484.

51.   Ibid.

52.   Ibid., p. 479. I am indebted to Michael Haykin for this insight. See his work, Michael G. Haykin, *Rediscovering the Church Fathers* (Wheaton, IL: Crossway, 2011).

through His own Spirit His wisdom which is ordained unto our glory. It is God who grants efficacy to our labors.'[53] The very purpose of good works demonstrates the grace of God which is lacking in the merits of the individual. Thus, good works are in keeping with the disposition of humility as it is God who accomplishes His eternal will in the Christian's good work.

Basil's contribution to Evangelicalism

Basil's contributions to the Evangelical church are diverse, but applicable to the modern church era. His role as monastic reformer often is relegated to a history lesson but it is a lesson that should be reviewed, taught, and learned for modern Evangelicals.

Holiness in the church

The concern for purity in the fourth-century church was a key issue for Basil. The Constantinian edict that made it popular to be a church member allowed many people to join the church for political exigency. The numbers of people joining the church were staggering. The fact that Arianism was a constant threat meant that the church had not settled the issue of soteriology and Christology. The end result of the mass appeal to the church was that many new adherents simply were not saved.

The monastic movement helped the soul attain purity via a rigorous lifestyle dedicated to the Lord. The solace of the desert helped the soul to focus the mind and the emotions on the will of God. Thus, the monastic, in contradiction to the worldliness of the church, pursued the holiness of God. Basil saw the dichotomy between the attempt to attain purity for the soul and the lack of ministry to the church. This dichotomy was predicated upon the isolation of the monk.

The reform of Basil was an attempt to bring the commandment of the Lord back into proper focus within the ecclesia. The church membership is commanded to love the Lord and love

---

53. Basil, *Ascetical Works*, p. 479.

its neighbors. The isolation of monasticism did not allow the second part of the commandment to be observed. Basil's reform was designed to allow the monk to engage in ministry to the church while doing so in a holy manner. The end result is that the life of Christ is now witnessed through the lives of the church membership as the church at large has the living model to imitate. The monastic now demonstrates the character of purity so that the commands of the Lord are not hindered by an improper or sinful lifestyle.

This is a lesson that the modern church must revisit. The issue of purity in thought and deed is lacking in the twenty-first century ecclesia. The valid lesson is that the fourth-century church may provide the example to the twenty-first century church in lessons of holiness and purity. The way to revival can be learned from the fact that the modern church must not love the world but seek to discipline itself in order for the love of God to flourish.

The Moral Rules and The Large Asceticon

The *Moral Rules* and *The Large Asceticon* illustrated the discipline of the church body in order to use their spiritual gifts in relation to one another. The goal of these works was to provide focus to the individual members in order to seek holiness. This would allow the church to become the 'community of perfect Christians.'[54] The pattern of conformity is not to worldliness but to godliness. The quality of life and the holiness of life are to be the prevailing dispositions of each member in relation to one another.

The lesson for the twenty-first church is provided by the dissensions within the fourth-century church. As the early church had deep doctrinal and personal divisions, the leadership was able to demonstrate the necessary return to biblical authority in order to heal the factions within the church. The same must

---

54. Fedwick, *The Church and the Charisma of Leadership in Basil of Caesarea*, p. 99.

be true of the twenty-first century church. The contemporary ecclesia must hear Basil as he spoke to the anemic and worldly church. The claims of purity, discipline, and love for the brethren are based upon the holiness of God. The discipline of the body (individually and corporately) must be a reality so that the health of the ecclesia can embrace revival once again.

Holiness

Again, Basil was concerned about the morality of the church. He knew that the church must live godly through the Holy Spirit. His passion was to be a holy man of the Word but also to encourage the leadership to do the same. This issue was not to simply 'embrace certain orthodox notions'[55] but to live lives rooted in the soteriology, or doctrines of the salvation, of Christ. The holiness of God is attained though the humility of Christians as the glory of God is exalted individually and corporately in the ecclesia.

The twenty-first-century church desperately needs the lesson of Basil. Godliness is the solution to the worldly pettiness that has engulfed the contemporary church. The fundamental issue for the contemporary church is to seek God's glory via His presence in the church. The ecclesiastical compromise of worldliness and the attempt of the church to seek God's glory must be renounced as sinful. The church simply cannot live worldly and seek God's glory at the same time. That is paradoxical in nature and unscriptural in approach. Haykin remarked, 'True Christianity is both orthodoxy and orthopraxy.'[56] The doctrines of the Scriptures must be practiced in humility and holiness in order to enter God's glory. This theological concept must be revived within the church.

---

55. Haykin, *Rediscovering the Church Fathers*, p. 117.

56. Ibid.

4

DEVELOPMENT OF THE DOCTRINE
OF THE HOLY SPIRIT

Basil's contribution to the doctrine of the Holy Spirit (pneu-matology) was not produced in a vacuum. The fourth century certainly struggled with Christology but the afterthought of pneumatology soon came to the forefront of the second phase of Arianism. Philip Schaff stated, 'The decision of Nicaea, related primarily only to the essential deity of Christ. But in the wider range of the Arian controversies the deity of the Holy Ghost, which stands and falls with the deity of the Son, was indirectly involved.'[1] Although the Council of Nicaea did address Arian-ism successfully, the council did not have the lasting impact on the theology of the church as they might have assumed.

The Nicene Creed

The legacy of Nicaea is the Nicene Creed. This creed established the orthodox position of the consubstantiality of the Son to the Father. However, the creed only treated the Holy Spirit in an indirect manner. The famous ending of the creed has an appen-dix that states, 'And in the Holy Ghost.'[2] The beginning of the

---

1. Philip Schaff, *Nicene and Post-Nicene Christianity: From Constantine the Great to Gregory the Great A.D. 311-590*, vol. 3 of *History of the Christian Church* (Peabody, MA: Hendrickson Publishers, 2006), p. 663.

2. Philip Schaff, *The Creeds of Christendom*, vol. 1 (Grand Rapids, MI: Baker Book House, 1998), p. 29.

Creed is the confession of faith and starts with the phrase 'We believe in one God the Father almighty ... And in one Lord Jesus Christ.'[3] The creed expresses the issue of Christology but leaves much to be desired concerning the person of the Holy Spirit. Basically, the appendage to the creed left an uncertainty as to the classification of the third person of the Trinity. One may question whether or not the creed should be read to mean that all that applies to the Son applies to the Holy Spirit. One also may question if it should be taken at face value that the Holy Spirit is divine but not personal.

> **Nicene Creed:** This creed was the result of the First Ecumenical Council of Nicea in A.D. 325. That council affirmed the consubstantiality of the Son with the Father. The Nicene Creed was an attempt to deal with Arianism, which denied the consubstantiality of Father and Son. The Nicene Creed became the orthodox position, as was upheld at the Council of Constantinople in 381, thereby sealing the final and decisive victory for the orthodox party.

The lack of clarification allowed the resurgence of theological speculation. Macedonius, a moderate semi-Arian, and leader of the Pneumatomachi, propagated the status of the Holy Spirit as being created but did allow for the consubstantiality of the Son. Thus, for the next forty years this controversy raged throughout the Empire and the church.

The question of 'how' the semi-Arians regained standing in the church and Empire should be examined in order to understand Basil's lifelong controversy with them. The resurgence of Arianism is related directly to the changing imperial matters of the state.

The Arian resurgence

Within two years of the Nicene Council, Eusebius of Caesarea was able to depose Eustathius of Antioch along with five other bishops throughout Syria and Palestine. The key issue that Eusebius used

---

3.   Schaff, *The Creeds of Christendom*, p. 27.

for support was the accusation that Eustathius made 'sarcastic and offensive comments about the Empress Helena, when she made a pilgrimage to the Holy Land following the tragic events in her family'.[4] As a result, Eustathius was a deposed bishop with the approval of Constantine. In addition, Arius' misfortune had changed for the better. Behr wrote:

> On November 27, 327, Constantine wrote to Arius, expressing surprise that he had not shown himself at court and summoning him to appear, with a view to Arius' returning to his home country. Arius, together with Euzoius, submitted a statement of faith to Constantine which describes the Son as being 'begotten from the Father before all ages,' but remaining silent about the *homoousios*.[5]

As a result, Arius was received back into communion at Alexandria.

Constantine's actions prompted Eusebius of Nicomedia and Theognis of Nicaea to appeal to the Emperor for reception back into the church. By the end of A.D. 327, the leaders of the Arian party were welcomed back into the church. A most unfortunate event occurred the next year with the death of Alexander of Alexandria. The church turned to Athanasius for leadership. However, he had trouble with the Arians from the beginning. Athanasius refused to admit Arius back into the church. The Arians, even though armed with political backing, were frustrated with Athanasius. Michael Davies wrote, 'It soon became clear that under no circumstances would the young Patriarch compromise orthodoxy, even to please the Emperor, and so his enemies initiated the campaign of calumny and persecution against him which would last till his death.'[6]

---

4. Behr, *The Nicene Faith*, vol. 2., pp. 69-70.

5. Ibid., p. 70.

6. Michael Davies, *Saint Athanasius: Defender of the Faith* (Kansas City, MO: Angelus Press, 2001), p. 7. Athanasius was banished five times throughout his ministry. Thus the church was threatened constantly with Arian emperors and Arian bishops. The statement that the whole world was against Athanasius was somewhat correct. However, in response Athanasius stated, '*Athanasius Contra Mundum* – Athanasius against the World.'

Athanasius found himself embroiled in the battle with the Arians in the 350s although much of his ministry was spent in exile. However, he realized that there was little fundamental difference between the *homoiousians* and the orthodox party. Robert Letham wrote, 'According to the homoiousians, the Son is like the Father, with full divinity and personal distinction.'[7] Kelly stated, 'So in his *De Synodis* (359) Athanasius made a conciliatory gesture, saluting the Homoeousians (same as homoiousian) as brothers who in essentials were at one with himself.'[8]

Athanasius took another initiative toward unity at the death of Constantius. In 362 at the council of Alexandria, which he chaired, he led the council to recognize that the issue of language had to be dealt with. According to Kelly, this council decided:

> What mattered was not the language used but the meaning underlying it. Thus the formula 'three hypostasis', hitherto suspect to the Nicenes because it sounded in their ears painfully like 'three ousiai,' i.e., three divine beings, was pronounced legitimate provided it did not carry on the Arian connotation of 'utterly distinct, alien hypostasis, different in substance from each other', in other words, 'three principles of three Gods', but merely expressed the separate subsistence of the three persons in the consubstantial Triad.[9]

The conclusion of this council shocked many but it did bring the Orthodox Nicene party together with the Homoiousian party, thereby making it the majority throughout the eastern and western churches. As Kelly depicted, this union allowed the emergence of the 'one ousia, three hypostasis' formula that would become the standard slogan of orthodoxy.[10]

---

7. Robert Letham, *The Holy Trinity* (Phillipsburg, NJ: P&R Publishing, 2004), p. 124.

8. Kelly, *Early Christian Doctrine*, pp. 252-3.

9. Ibid., pp. 253-4. This council so angered Julian that he banished Athanasius for a fourth time.

10. Kelly, *Early Christian Doctrines*, pp. 253-4.

Athanasius' contribution to the doctrine of the Holy Spirit

Forty years after Nicea, Serapion of Thimuis asked Athanasius to review the role of the Holy Spirit within the Trinity. The occasion for this request revealed the confusion concerning the nature and role of the Holy Spirit. Responding to Serapion's letter, Athanasius stated:

> For you were clearly upset, my beloved and truly most dear friend, and you wrote that certain ones who have withdrawn from the Arians on account of their blasphemy against the Son of God have nonetheless set their minds against the Holy Spirit, claiming not only that he is a creature but also that he is one of the ministering spirits (Heb 1:14) and is different from the angels only in degree.[11]

This request demonstrated that the person of the Holy Spirit was becoming a topic of concern but also caused confusion regarding the nature of the Trinity. The issue at hand was a hermeneutical problem. Thus, Athanasius addressed the problematic issue by stating that the opponents of the Holy Spirit used a 'certain mode of exegesis'[12] or *tropikoi*, as stated in the Greek.[13]

Tropikoi: This word is a derivative of tropology or trope and is very similar to typology. The technical term referred to a heretical group who were members of Serapion's church. That particular group used figurative expressions and figures of speech to distort the meaning of the Scriptures, especially in reference to the deity of the Holy Spirit.

11. Athanasius, *Letters to Serapion on the Holy Spirit* (Yonkers, NY: St. Vladimir's Seminary Press, 2011), p. 53.

12. Ibid., p. 54.

13. Athanasius used the term without defining the term. The rationale for this approach is that Serapion understood the term and thus explanation is not needed. For modern acumen, the term may mean 'Misinterpreters,' or 'Spirit-fighters.' See *Works on the Spirit* (Yonkers, NY: St. Vladimir's Seminary Press, 2011), p. 21, for this discussion. Lewis Ayers, *Nicaea and Its Legacy* (Oxford, UK: Oxford University Press, 2004), p. 212, indicates that the *Tropikoi* 'appears to be an isolated phenomenon.'

Date of the work

The *Letters to Serapion* was thought to be the first work produced on the Holy Spirit. Letham stated, '*Athanasius's Letters to Serapion on the Holy Spirit* are the first extensive treatment of the Holy Spirit in the history of the church, written between 355 and 360 and antedating Basil the Great's famous treatise.'[14] If Robert Letham is correct, Athanasius penned this work during his third exile.[15] The third exile was between the years 355 and 361, which is an early date for the work.

Recently, there has been speculation that Didymus the Blind's work, *On the Holy Spirit*,[16] may have been written at the same time or shortly after the Athanasius treatment. The evidence is lengthy and requires serious consideration, of which this volume does not allow. However, one piece of evidence, the internal content of Didymus' *On the Holy Spirit*, should be considered. Lewis Ayers reasoned that Didymus was responding to Eunomius' *Apology* 'which was most likely delivered at the Council of Constantinople in January 361 and published in that year or the next'.[17] This allowed for the fact

---

14. Letham, *The Holy Trinity*, p. 141.

15. Athanasius' third exile occurred in the year 355. His writings and preaching in defence of the orthodox faith proved unpopular as the Arians still had a firm relationship with Constantius, who was sole Emperor of the Empire after the assassination of Constans (his brother) and the vanquishing of Maxentius. George Dragas, *Saint Athanasius of Alexandria: Original Research and New Perspectives* (Rollinsford, NH: Orthodox Research Institute, 2005), p. 201, wrote, 'His (Constantius) political victory supported his intention to turn against the Orthodox and especially Athanasius who was supported by Maxentius. Athanasius was called to appear before the Emperor. He refused, and, instead, addressed to the Emperor his *Apology to Constantius*.' Athanasius subsequently was exiled for the third time. This exile lasted from 355 to 361.

16. Didymus the Blind, *On the Holy Spirit* (Yonkers, NY: St. Vladimir's Seminary Press, 2011).

17. Andrew Radde-Gallwitz, 'Introduction,' *On the Holy Spirit* (Yonkers, NY: St. Vladimir's Seminary Press, 2011), p. 40. Radde-Gallwitz quoted Lewis Ayers, 'The Holy Spirit as Undiminished Giver: Didymus the Blind's *De Spiritu Sancto* and the Development of Nicene Pneumatology,' pp. 57-72 in Janet Rutherford and Vincent Twomey, eds., *The Holy Spirit in the Fathers of the Church: The Proceedings of the Seventh International Patristic Conference*, Maynooth, 2008 (Dublin: Four Courts Press, 2011).

that the semi-Arians, through the writings of Eunomius, had pervasive influence upon the eastern Mediterranean.

The rationale for the above approach is that Didymus alluded to John 5:19 and 16:14 which are the same Scriptures that Eunomius utilized. If that is the case, then the date of *On the Holy Spirit* cannot be prior to 361 or 362. This parallels with Basil's work, *Against Eunomius*, especially since both Basil and Didymus reviewed Amos 4:13 and John 1:13. In order to access the timeframe, one should keep the dates of each work in mind. Remember that Basil's work (*Against Eunomius*) is dated 362–3 and possibly as late as 364. Andrew Radde-Gallwitz noted, 'These verses appear together in both works (Basil and Didymus) and not in Athanasius. In a number of ways, Basil and Didymus interpret the verses similarly, while differing from Athanasius' treatment of the verses in the *Letters to Serapion*.'[18] This may mean that Basil, while writing *Against Eunomius*, was aware of Didymus' work.

Even if one argued that Basil was dependent upon or influenced by Didymus, the argument is not sustained easily. For example, it would be quite natural for both men to work with the same Scriptures that Eunomius utilized if both were writing against a common work. Thus, the internal evidence of Basil and Didymus does not prove dependency or influence of one upon the other necessarily.[19]

Regardless, the fact that Didymus may have responded to Eunomius (and Basil being aware of Didymus) would place *On the Holy Spirit* in the mid 364–5 time period. Consequently, Didymus responded to the same Arian crisis as Basil, which allows an earlier dating than previously thought. If the dating of Didymus is correct, then the new date also reveals how significantly the second phase of Arianism had taken root in the church during this time.

---

18. Radde-Gallwitz, *Introduction*, pp. 41-2.

19. Mark DelCogliano concluded that Basil was aware of Didymus' work. See 'Basil of Caesarea, Didymus the Blind, and the Anti-Pneumatomachian Exegesis of Amos 4:13 and John 1:13,' in *Journal of Theological Studies* 61 (2010), pp. 644-58.

An additional thought concerning the relationship of Didymus to Athanasius should be recognized. A dependency or influence of one upon the other does not seem to exist. In other words, Basil might have been aware of Didymus but that does not mean that Athanasius was aware of Didymus. Radde-Gallwitz stated, 'With respect to the dating question, Athanasius demonstrates no awareness of Didymus and emphasizes the novelty of his opponents; thus, we should not expect Didymus's work to be significantly earlier than Athanasius.'[20] Given the above argument, it is unlikely that Didymus wrote his work prior to Athanasius. There does not seem to be a dependency of Didymus upon Athanasius, even though a case can be made that Basil was aware of Didymus while writing against the common work of Eunomius.

The revealing issue to be considered is that Arianism was, once again, at the forefront of the theology of the church. To dismiss Arianism as a minor problem limited to a small geographical area is to overlook the work of God in such men as Basil, Didymus, and Athanasius.

The content

There are three letters that comprise the work of *Letters to Serapion*. The content of the first letter focuses on the consubstantiality of the Spirit within the Trinity. The second letter summarizes the doctrine of the Son in relation to the Father. This allowed Athanasius to demonstrate that the Holy Spirit is proper to the Son as the Son is proper to the Father. Letter Three is an abridgement of the first letter.

Letter 1

In the second section[21] of the letter, Athanasius connected the teachings of the Tropikoi with Arianism. He stated their 'kind of thinking is not foreign to the Arians.'[22] His rationale is that as

---

20. Radde-Gallwitz, *Introduction*, p. 37.

21. The remainder of this work will follow the outline of Athanasius, *Letters to Serapion on the Holy Spirit* (Yonkers, NY: St. Vladimir's Seminary Press, 2011). This book contains sectional numbers for references which will be utilized for clarity.

22. Athanasius, *Letters to Serapion*, 1.2.1.

they have denied the Son they now deny the divinity of the Holy Spirit. Athanasius stated, 'By dividing the Spirit from the Word they no longer preserve the divinity of the Trinity as one, but rupture it, and mix with it a nature that is foreign to it and different in kind, and reduce it to the level of creatures.'[23] R. P. C. Hanson concurred as he wrote, 'Now, as Athanasius has abandoned the desire to see any mediating element within the Godhead nor any mediating supernatural instrument used to come between God and men, except the human nature of Jesus Christ, he cannot allow the createdness of the Holy Spirit.'[24]

The conclusion of the Tropikoi was that the Holy Spirit is a creature, which they based upon Amos 4:13. They deemed the word *spirit* to mean the Holy Spirit. Athanasius used the argument that the word *spirit* is unqualified or undetermined. For the Spirit-fighters, the Amos passage became a proof-text in which to appeal in order to denounce the deity of the Holy Spirit. Hanson went so far as to say, 'Under the magical wand of mistranslation it became a Trinitarian formula which included a created Holy Spirit.'[25]

Athanasius gave Scriptural examples that disprove the alleged Trinitarian formula. For example, he cited Isaiah 7:2 and Jonah 1:4. In both passages, the word *spirit* is used but does not refer to the Holy Spirit. The Tropikoi also used Zechariah 4:5 to depict that the angel speaking to Zechariah was the Holy Spirit. Athanasius responded that they misunderstood the passages, stating that the context clearly explained that the angel and the Holy Spirit are two different entities. This allowed Athanasius to categorize the Holy Spirit as divine by revealing that he is 'proper to the Word'.[26] Alvyn Pettersen commented on Athanasius' use of the word *proper*:

---

23. Athanasius, *Letters to Serapion*, 1.2.3.

24. R. P. C. Hanson, *The Search for the Christian Doctrine of God: The Arian Controversy* 318–81 (Edinburgh, Scotland: T&T Clark, 1988), p. 749.

25. Ibid., pp. 749-50.

26. Athanasius, *Letters to Serapion*, 1.11.4.

When then Athanasius uses 'proper' of the Son's and Spirit's relation to the Father, he does so to stress their correlativity with the Father, and their common distinction from creation, to which the divine Creator, although Creator and Sustainer, is essentially 'eternal,' 'foreign,' or 'alien.' Hence repeatedly, Athanasius notes that the Son is 'not foreign', but proper to the Father's essence. Equally Athanasius argues that the Spirit is not 'alien to the Son's nature nor to the Father's Godhead' but in essence proper to the Son and *proper* to the Father's Godhead.[27]

Pettersen made the point that by using the word *proper*, Athanasius denounced the concept of an Arian created Holy Spirit. Pettersen continued:

The term *proper* serves then to stress that the Son and Spirit are as closely related to the Father as characteristics are to their natural subjects, as radiance to light, and streams to fountains. Yet the Son and Spirit are not therefore but characteristics, however proper, of the Father. The Logos is the Father's Offspring and Image; the Spirit is the Father's Spirit ... By the term *proper* Athanasius seeks to retain both the indivisibility of the one Triad and the eternity of the very Father, very Son and very Spirit.[28]

Thus, as Pettersen correctly identified, Athanasius based his understanding of the Holy Spirit as being a member of the Trinity and not of the created order.

Athanasius made this point by distinguishing created angels in comparison to the Holy Spirit who does not belong to the same category. For example, Athanasius asked in rhetorical fashion, 'Who from among all the angels is to be ranked with the Trinity? For indeed they are all of them not one in number! Which of them descended to the Jordan in the form of a dove?'[29] The seemingly obvious answer is that an angel did not perform

---

27. Alvyn Pettersen, *Athanasius* (London, EN: Geoffrey Chapman, 1995), p. 145.

28. Ibid., p. 146.

29. Athanasius, *Letters to Serapion*, 1.11.4.

these functions but God the Holy Spirit did minister these functions. The point is that the Holy Spirit belongs to the Trinity and not to creation. Bobrinskoy stated, 'Either the Spirit is a creature and there is no Trinity, because the Trinity cannot be the sum of the divinity (the Father and the Son) and the creature (the Holy Spirit), or God is Trinity and the Spirit is consubstantial with the Father.'[30]

The Spirit being consubstantial with the Father has direct implications on soteriology, the theology of salvation. The soteriology of God was always the concern of Athanasius. Therefore, he revealed that if the Holy Spirit is not consubstantial with the Father then salvation is not possible. Athanasius asked, 'Who will join you to God if you do not have the Spirit of God himself but the spirit of the created order?'[31] The point is that salvation is unattainable if the work of God is performed by a created being. Since the Trinity involves the mutual indwelling (*perichoresis*) of all three members, the work of God, via the ministry of salvation, is of the Trinity. Letham stated this truth as he wrote, 'The perichoretic relations of the three persons underlie their inseparable involvement in the one work of God our salvation.'[32]

After reviewing the soteriology of the Trinity, Athanasius concluded the first letter by appealing to the traditional faith of the apostles and the witness of the Scriptures. He noted, 'What I have handed on accords with the Apostolic faith that the Fathers handed down to us. I have not made anything up that falls outside of it, but have written only what I learned in harmony with the Holy Scriptures.'[33] Athanasius understood that the revelation of the Trinity is from the Scriptures and not external sources. His position is that the orthodox faith, which includes soteriology, is centered upon the testimony and revelation of the

---

30. Bobrinskoy, *The Mystery of the Trinity*, p. 224.

31. Athanasius, *Letters to Serapion*, 1.29.2.

32. Letham, *The Holy Trinity*, p. 142.

33. Athanasius, *Letters to Serapion*, 1.33.2.

Holy Scriptures and thus, properly interpreted, they are reliable
for doctrinal formulation.[34] The thrust of the argument is difficult to overlook: if the Trinity is not embraced per the revelation
of the Scriptures, the church has been in error concerning soteriology. However, the universal witness of the church conforms to
the revelation of the Scriptures (i.e., that God as Trinity secures
the salvation of humanity). That is the witness and confession
of the church based upon the revelation of the Holy Scriptures.

Letter 2

The occasion of the second letter was to have a brief theological statement at the request of Serapion. In sections 2.1.1–2.9.3,
Athanasius argued that the Son is from the Father and of one being with the Father. He demonstrated that the Son is ontologically
the same as the Father and that the relationship existed eternally.
Thomas F. Torrance stated:

> Athanasius went on to point out that after having fulfilled his
> human economy, the Incarnate Son now sits at the right hand
> of the Father and the Father in him, as always was and is forever.
> That is to say, Athanasius insisted that the union between the In-
> carnate Son and the Father, far from being merely a transient epi-
> sode in time, is ontologically and eternally real in the Godhead.[35]

Athanasius echoed the Nicene Creed that the Son is eternally
the Son of the eternal Father. The second section of the letter
(2:10.1–2.13.3) addressed the relationship between the Spirit
and the Son. Athanasius stated, 'For we will find the way in
which we know the Son belongs to the Father corresponds to
the way in which the Spirit belongs to the Son.'[36] By affirming
the unity of the Son to the Father and the Spirit to the Son,
Athanasius affirmed the unity of the Trinity. Dragas stated, 'The

---

34. Athanasius, *Letters to Serapion*, 1.32.1.

35. Thomas F. Torrance, *Trinitarian Perspectives* (Edinburgh, Scotland: T&T Clark,
    1994), p. 13.

36. Athanasius, *Letters to Serapion*, 2.10.2.

integrity and wholeness of the divine nature suggest that in his generation the divine Son is not a part of the Father's being, but he is integral to it, a total image and effulgence of the Father's being ... The principle which applies to the Father-Son relation also applies to the Son-Spirit and Father-Spirit relations.'[37] The point made is that the Holy Spirit inheres in the Trinity on the same basis as the Son. The theological motif is that since the Son is one with the Father, so is the Spirit. This concept establishes the deity of the Holy Spirit and denounces the false concept that the Holy Spirit is a creature.

Athanasius understood the work of grace was at stake if the Holy Spirit is nothing more than a creature. He wrote, 'But if it has been confessed that the Son is not a creature because he is in the Father and the Father in him, then there is every necessity that the Spirit is not a creature. For the Son is in him, and he is in the Son. Therefore, whoever receives the Spirit is called the temple of God.'[38] The soteriology of God deteriorates if the Holy Spirit is deemed other than God. The Trinity cannot function with a creature, which means that salvation is impossible. On the positive side, if one receives the Son and the process is because of the work of the Spirit, then salvation is accomplished. Thus, in order to receive the salvation of the Son, one must accept the work and role of the Holy Spirit.

The last section of the letter, 2.13.4–2.16.4, focused on the Spirit's role in the common activity of the Trinity. Athanasius examined the argument of the Tropikoi and depicted their logical conclusion. He stated, 'If the Spirit is a creature, and if creatures come from nothing, it is clear that there was a point when the Trinity was not a Trinity but a dyad.'[39] The end result is that the Trinity is not eternal but established by a 'process of change and progress.'[40] In reviewing the

---

37. Father George Dion Dragas, *Athanasiana: Essays in the Theology of Saint Athanasius* (London, 1980), p. 69.

38. Athanasius, *Letters to Serapion*, 2.12.4.

39. Ibid., 2.16.1.

40. Ibid.

logical conclusion of this position, Athanasius informed the reader that the church never has proclaimed such a notion. In fact, the Trinity is the foundation of the church!

Letter 3

The tone of this letter revealed the frustration of Athanasius concerning the Tropikoi and consequently is less conciliatory than the previous two letters. Apparently, Serpion sent another letter asking for clarification from Athanasius on the relationship between Father and Holy Spirit. The Tropikoi asked the question, 'If the Holy Spirit is not a creature then is he a son?'[41] This is no mere question though, as Athanasius recognized the argument that Serapion had revealed to him. Athanasius wrote, 'Then, as you write, they add: "If the Spirit shall receive from (John 16:14) the Son, and is given from him (for so it is written)" they immediately draw the conclusion: "then is the Father a grandfather, and the Spirit his grandson."'[42]

Athanasius did not think that the Tropikoi were sincere in their reasoning.[43] However, he proceeded to answer the question. First, he asked rhetorically, 'Where is the Spirit called a son?'[44] Athanasius did not allow this rhetoric to be unanswered. He said, 'In the Scriptures the Spirit is not called Son but Holy Spirit and Spirit of God. Just as the Spirit is not called Son, so too it is not written that the Son is the Holy Spirit.'[45] The point being that the Holy Spirit and the Son are distinct from one another as the names of each member of the Trinity indicate.

Athanasius continued by stating that the Tropikoi cannot interchange the names, which means there is no mutability within the Trinity. In other words, the Father is not a grandfather

---

41.   Athanasius, *Letters to Serapion*, 3.1.3.

42.   Ibid., 3.1.3.

43.   Ibid., 3.2.1 He questioned if the Tropikoi were Christians!

44.   Ibid., 3.2.5.

45.   Ibid., 3.2.4.

and the Son will never become a father. His rationale is that the relationships and the persons of the Trinity are eternal. Athanasius explained, 'It is not permitted to exchange the names of this faith: the Father is always the Father, and the Son is always the Son, and the Holy Spirit is and is said to be always the Holy Spirit.'[46] Theodore C. Campbell commented, 'The relationships are absolute, outside of time, and intrinsic to the being of God. The eternal stability of the Godhead does not change within itself, as the Father becoming a grandfather and the Son becoming a father, etc., would suggest. The names of Father, Son, and Spirit are to be retained as they stand because they point to stable relations within the Godhead.'[47] The purpose was for Athanasius to demonstrate that the Trinity is eternal, which means the members are eternal in relationship, role, and function. Thus, the Tropikoi confused the Trinitarian relationships simply because they confused the nature and roles of each member of the Trinity.

One final issue is noteworthy concerning Athanasius' work, *Letters to Serapion on The Holy Spirit*. Athanasius anticipated the future controversy known as the *Filioque clause*.[48]

Filioque clause: The word *Filioque* is a Latin word meaning 'and from the Son.' It is found in the western versions of the Nicene Creed in the section that refers to the Holy Spirit. It asserts that the Holy Spirit proceeds from both Father and Son. The word was not in the original formulation of the Nicene Creed, but added in order to bring clarity to the relationships between Father, Son and Holy Spirit. The *Filioque clause* was a source of dissension between the eastern and western church. The dissension over the clause finally led to the division of the Greek eastern and the Latin western church in A.D. 1054. The division produced the Greek Orthodox Church and the Latin Roman Catholic Church.

---

46. Athanasius, *Letters to Serapion*, 3.6.4.

47. Theodore C. Campbell, 'The Doctrine of the Holy Spirit in the Theology of Athanasius,' *Scottish Journal of Theology* 27 (1974): 431.

48. See Chapter Two, footnote 72.

The sending of the Holy Spirit by the Father and receiving from the Son allowed Athanasius to demonstrate the congruent, eternal work of the Trinity. Again, Campbell commented on *Letters*, when he said, 'The Spirit's procession from the Father is seen in his mission from the Son, for as the Spirit is from the Son in mission, his is (or proceeds) from the Father.'[49] Campbell acknowledged that Athanasius understood the Son as giving the Spirit his mission/ministry to the world and church. Since Athanasius was not commenting on procession, the issue became difficult to place him as a double processionist.[50] For that matter, Thomas Torrance stated that Athanasius so emphasized the Godhead that:

> The Athanasian doctrine of the complete coinherence of the Father, the Son and the Holy Spirit in one another, and of the Monarchy as essentially Trinitarian, has the effect of cutting behind the problem of the *filioque* unecumenically added in the West to the Creed. In this Trinity no Person is before or after Another, no Person is greater or less, but all three Persons are coeternal and coequal in their substantive relations with one another.[51]

Letham agreed with Torrance as he observed, 'Later disagreements over the procession of the Holy Spirit might have been avoided if sufficient attention had been paid to his *Letters to Serapion*.'[52]

Didymus the Blind

The work, *On The Holy Spirit*, by Didymus, may have been written by 365, which is earlier than previously thought.[53] The recipients of the letter are stated within the work itself. Didymus stated:

---

49. Theodore C. Campbell, 'The Doctrine of the Holy Spirit in the Theology of Athanasius,' p. 434.

50. By using the term double processionist, this term appeals to the concept that the Son also sends the Spirit. Athanasius was not concerned about the issue primarily because it did not arise within the pneumatological conflict of his day.

51. Torrance, *Trinitarian Perspectives*, p. 20.

52. Letham, *The Holy Trinity*, p. 143.

53. See the discussion above.

> Nonetheless, some have raised themselves up to investigate heav-
> enly matters by a kind of recklessness rather than by living rightly,
> and they brandish certain things concerning the Holy Spirit which
> are neither read in the Scriptures nor taken from any of the old ec-
> clesiastical writers. And so, we are compelled to acquiesce to the oft-
> repeated exhortation of the brothers that we set forth our opinion
> on the Holy Spirit by means of proof-texts from the Scriptures ...[54]

Didymus was aware of the pneumatological issue concerning the deity of the Holy Spirit. He did not name those who have devi-ant opinions concerning the Holy Spirit but did state they have their information external of the Scriptures (and external of the older works on the Scriptures).

Two additional items should be noted before an exposition of Didymus' work is examined. Although he was aware of the deviant teaching on the Holy Spirit, he wrote his work at the request of 'the brothers.' This request may have been from his students at the academy in which he taught or it may have been from local priests in or near Alexandria, or perhaps even both. The point to be emphasized is that Didymus was regarded as a theologian that could address such weighty matters.

The other item to be noted is that Didymus stated his approach to demonstrate the deity of the Holy Spirit. He said that he would pro-vide proof-texts. In the modern Evangelical world, this approach has become associated with a deficient methodology. However, the reader should not read a twenty-first century meaning into a fourth-century term. By using the phrase 'proof-text,' Didymus simply meant he would show proof from the Scriptures that the Holy Spirit is divine.

The Spirit's nature and activity
In sections 3–9, Didymus examined the Scriptural content to introduce the Holy Spirit's divinity as the prologue to the work.[55] He mentioned only a few with the following caveat:

---

54. Didymus the Blind, *On The Holy Spirit*, p. 2.

55. This work will follow the references of *On The Holy Spirit* (Yonkers, NY: St. Vladi-mir's Seminary Press, 2011).

The books of the Divine Scriptures are filled with such statements [referring to the designated term, Holy Spirit, addition
for clarity mine]. But for the moment I have refrained from
enumerating the bulk of them in the present work because it is
easy for each reader to discover similar statements for himself
on the basis of those we have cited here.[56]

Therefore, the Scriptures reveal the Spirit as Holy, which means
that He is divine. The deity of the Holy Spirit is announced
in the Scriptures, which illustrates Didymus' view of the Holy
Bible. He did not reject traditions or councils but his foremost
appeal was the Scriptures themselves.

When he discussed the nature of the Holy Spirit, he stated that
the phrase 'Holy Spirit' refers to a definite person that belongs to
the Trinity. His ministry of sanctification yields the evidence that
the Holy Spirit is a tangible reality that is not a mere corporeal
substance. Didymus stated, 'This substance we are now discussing
produces wisdom and sanctification.'[57] Sanctification is produced
by the filling of the Spirit. Didymus referred to the filling of the
Holy Spirit as further evidence that the Holy Spirit is divine and
immutable. The Scriptures never indicate that a person is filled
with another creature, but with a Spirit.

For Didymus, the concept of sanctification places the Holy Spirit
in the Trinity and not among the created order. Again, he stated:

Therefore, if the Holy Spirit is the sanctifier, then it is evident
that his substance is not mutable but rather immutable. Now
the Divine Discourses report in the clearest possible way that
immutability of substance belongs to God alone and to his
only-begotten Son, even as they proclaim that every creaturely
substance is changeable and mutable. Therefore, since it has been
shown that the substance of the Holy Spirit is not changeable but
unchangeable, he will not be *homoousios* with a creature.[58]

56. Didymus the Blind, *On the Holy Spirit*, p. 5.

57. This work will follow the references of *On the Holy Spirit* (Yonkers, NY: St. Vladi-
    mir's Seminary Press, 2011), p. 11.

58. Didymus the Blind, *On the Holy Spirit*, p. 16.

Didymus appealed to the nature of the Holy Spirit as divine and immutable, which is the opposite of creation or created beings. The rationale is that the only beings that are immutable can be classified as God.

The issue of immutability also has the connotation that one can participate in God. Thus, creatures who are mutable, can participate in eternal life (immutability) because it is of the nature of God. Didymus made the logical case when he wrote:

> The substance of the Holy Spirit can be participated in and because of this, that he is uncreated. After all, immutability follows upon the capacity to be participated in, and eternity follows upon immutability. Conversely, mutability follows upon the capacity to participate, and being creatable follows upon mutability. Therefore, no created thing is immutable; for this reason, no created thing is eternal.[59]

The idea of participation involves the salvation of the creature. Eternal life is an entity that only God has and only God can give. Therefore, when the person is saved he or she has participated in God.

Didymus understood that the Holy Spirit gives the gift of salvation, filling, and other gifts, but is not diminished by His giving. Radde-Gallwitz stated, 'Didymus strongly emphasizes that only when we understand the Spirit to give without loss and to be immutable and omnipresent can we understand what it means for the Spirit to "fill" the apostles and Christians.'[60]

The ministry of gifting the believer is part of the Spirit's activity. Didymus pointedly stated that the Holy Spirit is active and distributing spiritual gifts to believers. He wrote in such a fashion as to contradict a heresy known as 'Spirit as activity.' According to Radde-Gallwitz, this position embraced the meaning that the

---

59. This work will follow the references of *On the Holy Spirit* (Yonkers, NY: St. Vladimir's Seminary Press, 2011), pp. 54-6.

60. Andrew Radde-Gallwitz, 'Introduction,' *On the Holy Spirit* (Yonkers, NY: St. Vladimir's Seminary Press, 2011), p. 46.

Holy Spirit was 'merely activity of God' and not a person.[61] Radde-Gallwitz also stated that the proponents of this position have not been identified.[62] Yet Didymus considered the problem of activity and personhood a viable issue for contention.

Didymus' use of 1 Corinthians 12 was to demonstrate that the Holy Spirit has a will that is consistent with Father and Son. Didymus stated:

> From this we learn that the nature of the Holy Spirit is active and 'distributing' (if I may speak thus). Accordingly, let us not be taken in by those who say that the Holy Spirit is an activity and not the substance of God. Many other passages also show that the nature of the Holy Spirit is subsistent, as in the passage that the Apostles write; *For it seemed good to the Holy Spirit and us* (Acts 15:28). For the expression *it seemed good* does not indicate an activity but a nature, especially since we also find something similar said about the Lord: as it seemed good to the Lord, so it was done (Job 1:21).[63]

The thrust of Didymus' review of 1 Corinthians 12 is, as previously stated, to indicate that the Spirit has a will and to emphasize the works (energy) of the Spirit.

By listing the 1 Corinthian 12 passage along with the Acts 15:28 Scripture, Didymus used the premise that 'if something is said to "seem good to the Spirit," then there must be a subsistent entity there with a will capable of approving it.'[64] Thus, by systematizing the Scriptures, Didymus proved that the Holy Spirit is a person who works in the 'common operations' of the Trinity.[65]

---

61. Andrew Radde-Gallwitz, 'The Holy Spirit as Agent, not Activity: Origen's Argument with Modalism and its Afterlife in Didymus, Eunomius, and Gregory of Nazianzus,' *Vigiliae Christianae* 65 (2011), p. 228. This article presents the argument that Didymus, Eunomius, and Gregory are not actually responding to a specific person but are 'using Origen's argument against modalism for their own purposes.'

62. Ibid., p. 228.

63. Didymus the Blind, *On the Holy Spirit*, p. 174.

64. Andrew Radde-Gallwitz, 'The Holy Spirit as Agent, not Activity: Origen's Argument with Modalism and its Afterlife in Didymus, Eunomius, and Gregory of Nazianzus,' p. 240.

65. Radde-Gallwitz, 'The Holy Spirit as Agent,' p. 241.

The Spirit: sent, procession, and name

In the last section of the work, Didymus reviewed the sending, procession, and name of the Holy Spirit. The issue of unity was the primary concern for Didymus. Therefore, he made the case that the sending of the Son was a Trinitarian act. However, the sending or procession of the Holy Spirit is in direct connection with His ministry to believers. Didymus wrote:

> The Spirit, who is Consoler, is sent from the Son, not in the way that the angels or the Prophets and Apostles are sent to minister, but as appropriate for the Spirit of God to be sent from Wisdom and Truth. After all, when the Son is sent from the Father, he is not separated and sundered from him, as he remains in him and has him in himself.[66]

The concept is that the Trinity is acting as one and not individually. The ministries of each member are separate and distinct but the action of each accord with the desire of God as Trinity.

Didymus demonstrated that the names of the Holy Spirit are based upon the Scriptures. The testimony of the Scriptures reveals the personal ministry of the Holy Spirit to believers but also demonstrates that the Trinity is active in the same ministry. Commenting on 2 Thessalonians 2:13, Didymus stated:

> Now in this passage, the gifts of God are best understood to exist in the Spirit, since one possesses faith and truth alike through the sanctification of the Spirit. Therefore, since our statements on these matters are right and pious and true, the terms 'holiness' and 'goodness' apply equally to the Father, Son, and Holy Spirit.[67]

Didymus' emphasis was upon the Trinity as the starting point for understanding the Father, Son, and Holy Spirit. Therefore, when specific ministry is accomplished by the Holy Spirit, it is performed in a Trinitarian act.

The conclusion of *On the Holy Spirit* is a warning not to commit the sin of blasphemy. The focal point of the work is to learn what was written and not blaspheme. Didymus clearly demonstrated a pious attitude toward the Trinity.

---

66. Didymus the Blind, *On The Holy Spirit*, p. 111.

67. Didymus the Blind, *On the Holy Spirit*, pp. 236-7.

Contribution to Evangelicalism

The historical review that helped shape the orthodox position of the Holy Spirit and the Trinitarian doctrine is valuable for the modern Evangelical. For example, the faith of these men to trust in the Scriptures when the combined opposition of theological and political forces united to thwart them is an example of incredible and credible faith. The easy approach would have been for Athanasius to capitulate to the current culture, then practice his theology in private isolation to ensure his own survival. Didymus simply could have chosen to remain in relative obscurity in the peace of Alexandria. However, both men had heaven on their hearts and the church on their minds and ventured into theological battle with the commitment that they served the God who called them to such a task.

The contribution of these men not only served the fourth century but still serves the twenty-first century. The recovery of the doctrine of the Trinity is a must if the church (local or universal) will have revival once again. The Trinitarian God works in unison to accomplish the goal of the world's redemption. The church must realize that the work of God in the fourth century still is needed in the twenty-first century. The very sustainability that Didymus and Athanasius grasped from the Lord still is available if the modern church would reclaim its doctrinal roots. The church must praise the Father, for the Son, through the Spirit.

One final contribution is noteworthy. Both of these men may have been writing for two different reasons but came to the same conclusion concerning the person of the Holy Spirit. The circumstances and audience were different but both men contributed theological wisdom and practical ministry to the church universally while addressing local situations. The wealth of these theological works is left for the modern Evangelical world to glean and harvest. The contemporary statistics reveal that many pastors feel isolated, yet the fourth-century example of two men giving back to the church meant that in spite of their burdens they were blessed greatly and were a blessing to their own generation. May the modern Evangelical world realize that the current ministry, in spite of personal heartache, can be a blessing to this generation.

BASIL'S CONTRIBUTION TO THE DOCTRINE
OF THE HOLY SPIRIT

Basil's earlier contribution to the development of the doctrine of the Holy Spirit, *Against Eunomius*, was written during A.D. 362-3. Approximately twelve years had passed and Basil had become the sole Bishop of Caesarea. The year was 374 and many issues had transpired in Caesarea but one of the foremost to keep in mind was that Basil had established himself as a theological force in the ecclesiastical affairs of the universal church. However, regardless of the previous work on the Holy Spirit, and in spite of the pastoral roles of Athanasius or Basil, the issue of Arianism simply did not go away into an obscure part of the Kingdom. Rousseau reviewed the period and concluded, 'Fresh developments had by now made it clear to Basil that his old essay [*Against Eunomius*] was no longer adequate.'[1]

Arianism in the Late 360s

Tarsus and the Pneumatomachians
In the year 369, Silvanus, the Bishop of Tarsus, and a personal friend of Basil, died and was succeeded by the Pneumatomachi.

---

1.   Rousseau, *Basil of Caesarea*, p. 263.

> **Pneumatomachians:** The term actually means *spirit-fighter*. There is speculation that the *Pneumatomachians* and the *Tropikoi* are the same group. However, the *Pneumatomachians* were eventually led by Eustathius of Sebaste after his differences with St. Basil. This group rejected the divinity of the Holy Spirit while accepting the consubstantiality of the Son.

Basil commented on this in his *Letter 34* sent to Eusebius of Samosata:

> Ah me! Tarsus is undone! This is a trouble grievous to be borne, but it does not come alone. It is still harder to think that a city so placed as to be united with Cilicia, Cappadocia, and Assyria should be lightly thrown away by the madness of two or three individuals, while you are all the while hesitating, settling what to do, and looking at one another's faces.[2]

The death of Silvanus and the emergence of the Pneumatomachi splintered the church into several factions. Jean Gribomont stated, 'The Majority, guided by Cyracus, held on to the moderate line of the deceased bishop. To the left, there were Arian tendencies. To the right, on the contrary, an anxious group, more demanding on the subject of Trinitarian orthodoxy, threatened to go into schism ... But this group, as well as the majority group, respected Basil.'[3] The rise of the heretics was quick and Basil characterized it as living in the days when the 'overthrow of the church seems imminent.'[4] The situation at Tarsus was one of many problems that forced Basil to reconsider the role of the Holy Spirit within the Trinity.

Eustathius of Sebaste

The second issue that came to the forefront was Eustathius of Sebaste. The friendship of both men became strained over the

---

2.   Basil, *Letter 34, Nicene and Post-Nicene Fathers*, 2nd Series, vol. 8, p. 136.

3.   Jean Gribomont, 'Intransigence and Irenicism in Saint Basil's "De Spiritu Sancto"' in *In Honor of Saint Basil the Great* (Still River, MA: St. Bede's Publications, 1979), pp. 116-17.

4.   Basil, *Letter 113, NPNF* 2nd Series, vol. 8, p. 189.

doctrine of the Holy Spirit. Eustathius had been a proponent of the Nicene Creed but was not willing to say that the Holy Spirit also was divine. According to Haykin, 'He was, for lack of a better term, committed to a subordinationist Binitarianism that was hostile to any conglorification of the Spirit with the Father and Son.'[5] Eustathius adhered to the position that the Holy Spirit was more of a gift for the believer.[6] Consequently, when he was pressed to define his position at a synod in 364, Eustathius commented, 'I can neither admit that the Holy Spirit is God, nor can I dare affirm him to be a creature.'[7] The fact that Eustathius was non-committal in his position on the Holy Spirit, and the fact that he associated with those who were of the Pneumatomachi, made him quite suspect concerning his theo-logical position on the role of the Holy Spirit. Basil's friendship with Eustathius would mean that Basil also would come under scrutiny.

In late 372, Theodotus of Nicopolis began to question the orthodoxy of Basil. Meletius of Antioch supported Theodotus and, thus, the call to Basil for clarity was demanded by two lead-ing bishoprics. Haykin noted:

> By the end of 372, Meletius and Theodotus were thus extremely suspicious of Eustathius' pneumatological views. The pneumatomachian environment around Eustathius only helped to give substance to their suspicions. Consequently, in late 372/early 373, Basil came under fire from his episcopal colleagues, especially Meletius and Theodotus, for his friendship with Eustathius.[8]

---

5.   Michael Haykin, *A Fence Around a Mystery: The Niceno-Constantinopolitan Creed, Its background and Teaching*, p. 10. This article was forwarded by its author. No publica-tion data is available for a complete bibliography entry.

6.   Haykin, *Rediscovering the Church Fathers*, p. 120.

7.   Socrates Scholasticus, *Church History Book II.45*, NPNF 2nd series vol. 2, p. 74.

8.   Michael Haykin, *The Spirit of God: The Exegesis of 1 & 2 Corinthians in the Pneumatom-achian Controversy of the Fourth Century* (Leiden, The Netherlands: E. J. Brill, 1994), pp. 35-6.

Indeed, Basil was under scrutiny for his own position. However, the call for clarity by Meletius also may have been an emotional heartbreak for Basil as he had supported Meletius as the rightful bishop of Antioch.[9]

Basil, ever the statesman, tried to reach an agreement with Eustathius that would provide peaceful closure to the situation. The occasion for Basil's outreach to Eustathius was provided by Theodotus at his invitation for Basil to join him at Nicopolis. Basil, on the way to the meeting with Theodotus, visited Eustathius at Sebaste in order to ascertain his position on the Holy Spirit. He met with Eustathius for two days in the summer of 373. Basil commented on his meeting:

> I put before him the accusations concerning the faith, advanced against him by our brother Theodotus, and I asked him, if he followed the right faith, to make it plain to me, that I might communicate with him; if he were of another mind, he must know plainly that I should be separated from him. We had much conversation on the subject, and all that day was spent in its examination; when evening came on we separated without arriving at any definite conclusion. On the morrow, we had another sitting in the morning and discussed the same points, with the addition of our brother Poemenius, the presbyter of Sebasteia, who vehemently pressed the argument against me. Point by point I cleared up the questions on which he seemed to be accusing me, and brought them to agree to my propositions. The result was, that, by the grace of the Lord, we were found to be in mutual agreement, even on the most minute particulars.[10]

Basil left the meeting with his old friend thinking they had resolved any misunderstanding on their pneumatology.

The result of the meeting was that Basil wrote a statement of faith for Eustathius to sign, affirming the orthodox position

---

9.   See Chapter Two for details.

10.   Basil, *Letter 99*, NPNF 2nd Series, vol. 8, p. 183.

(i.e., that the Holy Spirit is divine). Eustathius did sign the statement as recorded in *Letter 125*. The point Basil made in the letter was that the Holy Spirit is not created nor begotten. Basil stated:

> One point must be regarded as settled; and the remark is necessary because of our slanderers; we do not speak of the Holy Ghost as unbegotten, for we recognize one Unbegotten and one Origin of all things, the Father of our Lord Jesus Christ: nor do we speak of the Holy Ghost as begotten, for by the tradition of the faith we have been taught one Only-begotten: the Spirit of truth we have been taught to proceed from the Father, and we confess Him to be of God without creation ... I, Eustathius, bishop, have read to thee, Basil, and understood; and I assent to what is written above.[11]

Basil left the meeting with a signed statement of faith from Eustathius, affirming him as part of the orthodox movement. However, the euphoria of the accomplishment did not last long. Eustathius was supposed to reaffirm this document at a synod with Meletius and Theodotus present. However, he did not show up. For the next two years Eustathius condemned his own actions and slandered Basil as a Sabellian heretic. According to Haykin, 'Basil was so stunned by this turn of events and what amounted to the betrayal by a close friend that he kept silence until the winter of 374–375.'[12] Basil recounted his emotions in his own words as he wrote, 'I kept silence for my utter inability to say a word commensurate with my grief.'[13] Charles Frazee stated, 'The break between the two founders of asceticism in Anatolia was never healed.'[14] Basil had lost his friend, Eustathius.

---

11. Basil, *Letter 125*, pp. 195-6.

12. Haykin, *A Fence Around a Mystery*, p. 12.

13. Basil, *Letter 244.4*, p. 286.

14. Charles Frazee, 'Anatolian Asceticism in the Fourth Century: Eustathios of Sebastea and Basil of Caesarea,' *The Catholic Historical Review* 66:1 (Jan 1980), p. 32.

Opportunity from Amphilochius of Iconium

During the two-year interlude of silence, Basil became the mentor to Amphilochius, who eventually became the pastor at Iconium. Basil wrote:

> Walk before the people whom the Most High has entrusted to your hand. Like a skillful pilot, rise in mind above every wave lifted by heretical blasts; keep the boat from being whelmed by the salt and bitter billows of false doctrine; and wait for the calm to be made by the Lord so soon as there shall have been found a voice worthy of rousing Him to rebuke the winds and the sea ... You know that to a father's heart every time is suitable to embrace a well-loved son, and that affection is stronger than words.[15]

Basil had become the mentor and role model that every young pastor needs. He helped this young man establish his ministry at Iconium. Rousseau stated, 'So in these letters [to Amphilochius, also called the *Canonical Letters*], he gave advice on the church order to be followed in Iconium.'[16]

For the past three or four years, the battle with the Pneumatomachi had intensified. He had lost friends, opportunities, and had been forced into silence by the confusion within his own soul. The bitterness he felt may have subsided as Basil aided this young man in the ministry. His fatherly affection for this young man may have allowed Basil to revise his ministry for the church. For that matter, Gribomont called Amphilochius 'the first of Basil's disciples.'[17]

As Amphilochius was pastor at Iconium, the universal church on the world's stage still had to deal with the Pneumatomachi. The Arian position concerning the role of the Holy Spirit had ramifications for doxology within the church (i.e., how was the church to worship God). There is no surprise that the

---

15. Basil, *Letter 161.2*, pp. 214-15.

16. Rousseau, *Basil of Caesarea*, p. 260.

17. Gribomont, 'Intransigence and Irenicism,' p. 124.

Pneumatomachi allowed their theology to affect the doxology. In other words, since they did not attribute deity to the Holy Spirit, they did not worship Him as God in their ecclesiology. Thus, the doxology of the church was questioned.

The opportunity for Basil to reveal his personal theological convictions regarding the Holy Spirit came within the framework that he most delighted. Amphilochius sent a letter asking Basil to help him with the doxology of the church. Basil took the opportunity not only to help his young disciple, but also to help the doxology and worship practices of the church, while addressing the Arian pneumatology. His response to Amphiochius' request became his *magnum opus*, *On the Holy Spirit*.

Basil's *On the Holy Spirit*

The question at hand concerning the doxology was also an issue in Basil's own church. Basil admitted that he sometimes used different doxologies which may have led to confusion with his own people. He revealed:

> Lately while I pray with the people, we sometimes finish the doxology to God the Father with the form 'Glory to the Father *with* the Son, *together with* the Holy Spirit,' and at other times we use 'Glory to the Father *through* the Son *in* the Holy Spirit.' Some of those present accused us of using strange and mutually contradictory terms.[18]

Basil's alternate doxology ascribed glory to the Holy Spirit, which was tantamount to placing the Holy Spirit on the same theological plane as the Father and Son. On this note, J. N. D. Kelly demonstrated that Cyril also used the same concept as early as 358.[19] Basil defended his Trinitarian doxology and at the

---

18. Basil, *On the Holy Spirit* 1.3 (Crestwood, NY: St. Vladimir's Seminary Press, 1980), p. 17.

19. J. N. D. Kelly, *Early Christian Doctrines*, p. 256. This author is indebted to Howard Griffith, 'The Churchly Theology of Basil's *De Spiritu Sancto*,' *Presbyterion* 25:2 (1999), p. 93. Griffith revealed this issue in his journal article.

same time, set the doctrinal standard for pneumatological studies for the next one thousand years.[20]

Prepositions and deity

On the Holy Spirit has a unique structure in that it has a natural
breakdown into three parts which are divided easily into two
sections. The first and third parts form the first section as they
review the prepositions in relationship to the names of God as
revealed in the Scripture. This is the Bibliology section of the
work and it includes chapters 2 through 8, and 25 through 27.
However, the second part, which also forms the second section,
is more theological as Basil considered the Holy Spirit Himself
apart from the prepositions.[21] This section includes chapters 9
through 24, and 28 through 29.

The second section is actually the middle of the book and
divides the first section into two parts. In other words, there is
an A-B-A structure.[22]

First Section, Part One: Chapters 2–8

Chapters 2 through 8 are predicated upon the question of
proper worship in the church. Basil used the doxology as
a means to demonstrate distinction in personhood while
maintaining the unity of the Godhead. In chapter 2.4, he stated
that the opponents of orthodoxy follow the 'old trick invented
by Aetius' that 'things whose natures are dissimilar are expressed

---

20. Jaroslav Pelikan, 'The "Spiritual Sense" of Scripture; The Exegetical Basis for St.
Basil's Doctrine of the Holy Spirit,' in *Basil of Caesarea: Christian, Humanist, Ascetic:
A Sixteenth-Hundred Anniversary Symposium*, ed. Paul J. Fedwick (Toronto: Pontifi-
cal Institute of Medieval Studies, 1981), 1:337. Again, this writer is indebted to
Howard Griffith, 'The Churchly Theology of Basil's *De Spiritu Sancto*,' *Presbyterion*
25:2 (1999), p. 91.

21. Stephen M. Hildebrand, *The Trinitarian Theology of Basil of Caesarea* (Washington,
D.C.: The Catholic University of America Press, 2007), p. 179, closely follows this
outline. Slight deviation has occurred by adding *sections* and placing the three parts
of the work into two sections for clarity.

22. In order to have a systematic treatment, both parts one and three which form section one, will be considered together.

in dissimilar terms, and vice versa, dissimilar terms are used to describe things whose natures are dissimilar.'[23] For Aetius, the difference in the prepositions revealed the difference in the ontological nature of the Father and the Son. Thus, according to Aetius and his followers, they assigned the phrase *from whom* as belonging only to the Father and *through whom* as belonging only to the Son. The Holy Spirit was regulated by the phrase *in which*. Basil stated, 'They say that this assignment of prepositions must never be interchanged, in order that, as I have already said, one preposition phrase is always made to indicate a corresponding nature.'[24]

Basil continued, making the point that technical discussions of prepositions originated in pagan philosophers who were subordinationist in their thinking. Basil stated, 'Our opponents have first studied and admired these vain and empty distinctions, and then transferred them to the simple and uncluttered doctrine of the Spirit, using them to belittle God the Word and to deny the divine Spirit.'[25] He denounced the methodology of those who used rigid categories to express different natures within the Godhead. Basil continued, 'Now we admit that the Word of truth often uses these expressions in the manner just described, but we absolutely deny that the freedom of the Spirit is controlled by pagan pettiness.'[26]

Chapter 5 introduces the main proposal that Basil offered in his biblical treatment of prepositions. He stated, 'We shall now demonstrate our proposal: namely, that the Father does not accept *from whom* exclusively, and abandon *through whom* to the Son.'[27] To prove his point, Basil quoted both the Old and New Testaments to demonstrate that prepositions are used

23. Basil, *On the Holy Spirit*, 2.4, 18.

24. Ibid., 19.

25. Ibid., 3.5, 20.

26. Ibid., 4.6, 21.

27. Ibid., 5.7, 22.

interchangeably for the Godhead. He cited Romans 11:36,[28] stating that Paul uses both prepositions when referring to the Lord. Basil noted, 'The cause of being comes from Him to all things that exist, according to the will of God the Father.'[29] In a logical fashion, Basil demonstrated the absurdity of the rigid use of the prepositions. He wrote:

> If our opponents reject this interpretation, what argument will deliver them from openly falling into their own trap? If they will not permit these three expressions 'from whom,' 'through whom,' and 'in whom,' to be spoken concerning the Lord, they will be forced against their will to apply them to God the Father. Here their argument crumbles, because we find not only 'from whom' but also 'through whom' applied to the Father.[30]

Basil demonstrated that the use of prepositions is not limited to a specific member of the Godhead. Not only are the prepositions interchangeable but their meaning also interchanges from one subject to another. He quoted Genesis 4:1 referring to the preposition *through* as meaning the same as *from*. This demonstrates that the prepositions may change meaning due to their modification of differing subjects. The issue is that one cannot interpret prepositions so rigidly that the rules of grammar are strained.

Chapters 6 through 8 address the twin issues of ontological subordination and ontological equality. Chapter 6 once again takes up the theme of the doxology as described by Basil's opponents. Basil noted, 'Obviously they object because we finish the doxology by giving glory to the Father with the Only-begotten One, and do not exclude the Holy Spirit from this same glory.'[31] Basil reviewed their rationale by stating, 'They say that the Son is not equal to the Father, but comes after the Father. Therefore it

---

28. Romans 11:36: 'For from him and through him and to him are all things.'

29. Basil, *On the Holy Spirit*, 5.7, 23.

30. Basil, *On the Holy Spirit* 5.8, 24.

31. Ibid., 6.13, 28.

follows that glory should be ascribed to the Father *through* Him, but not *with* Him. *With* Him expresses equality but through Him indicates subordination.'[32]

Basil refuted this concept with a discussion on the word *after*. Basil asked, 'In what way do they say that the Son is after the Father? Is He later in time, or in rank, or in dignity?'[33] The issue is that one cannot conceive of the Father without the Son as if there was an interval in their relationship or existence. He quoted John 1:1 and focused upon the word *was* as settling the issue of the Son's eternality. Basil stated, 'No matter how far your thoughts travel backward, you cannot get beyond the *was*. No matter how hard you strain to see what is beyond the Son, you will find it impossible to pass outside the confines of the beginning. Therefore, true religion teaches us to think of the Son with the Father.'[34]

After establishing the equality of the Father and Son, Basil defended the use of two different doxologies, and their being received mutually by the church for worship. The differences in the doxologies depict how they are to be used and the rationale for their usage. He wrote:

> The Church recognizes both usages, dismissing neither as excluding the other. Whenever we reflect on the majesty of the nature of the Only-Begotten, and the excellence of His dignity, we ascribe glory to Him *with* the Father. On the other hand, when we consider the abundant blessings He has given us, and how He has admitted us as co-heirs into God's household, we acknowledge that this grace works for us *through* Him and *in* Him. Therefore, the best phrase when giving Him glory is *with whom* and the most appropriate for giving thanks is *through whom*.[35]

The rationale for the differing doxologies is determined by the purpose of the church at worship. If the purpose is to praise

32.   Basil, *On the Holy Spirit*

33.   Ibid., 6.14, 29.

34.   Ibid., 6.14, 30.

35.   Ibid., 7.16, 33.

God, then the doxology *through whom* is utilized to demonstrate that the worshiper's heart recognizes that the blessings of God come *through* the Son. However, the concept of worshiping the Son is demonstrated by using the phrase *with the Father.*

The glory of the Son is recognized as being the same glory of the Father. Basil defended the differing doxologies as not being just a tradition but by stating that the early Church Fathers followed the meaning of the Scriptures. Thus, he is convinced that the two different forms of praise are based scripturally.

Part One closes with chapter 8, which affirms the eternal nature of the Son to the Father. Basil united the person and works of the Godhead together, declaring their eternal equality when he stated, 'He is not different in essence, nor is He different in power from the Father, and if their power is equal, then their works are the same.'[36]

First Section, Part Three: Chapters 25–27

Part three of the book actually corresponds to the first part of the book as it relates to the same subject matter. Chapter 25 raises the issue that the prepositions are used interchangeably. However, Basil made the case that the doxology of his opponents is not biblical in that it cannot be found in the Scriptures. The same argument leveled against Basil by his opponents was being used against them. In this way, he justified using two different doxologies in the church at Caesarea.

Chapter 27 continues the argument with the support of tradition. He argued in Chapter 25 that neither doxology is found in Scripture. Thus, the origin of the doxology is from apostolic tradition. Concerning tradition, Basil wrote, 'We have received some from written sources, while others have been given to us secretly, through apostolic tradition.'[37]

The issue of tradition needs clarification. At first glance, it would appear that Basil had two equal authorities that governed

36. Basil, *On the Holy Spirit,* 8.19, p. 39.

37. Ibid., 27. 66, 98.

the church (i.e., the Scriptures and tradition). However, that simply is not the case. Basil was building on the time-honored concept that true hermeneutic was accomplished within the church. For that matter, an appeal to tradition was not to elevate an ecclesiastical consensus above the Scripture but to recognize 'tradition was, in fact, the authentic interpretation of Scripture ... Tradition was Scripture rightly understood.'[38] Cyril Karam concurred as he wrote, 'The doxology Basil is defending is ultimately rooted, therefore, in unwritten tradition which, with the doxology, conveys, in faith, its correct understanding.'[39] Another way of stating Basil's argument is that the letter of the Scriptures kills (or results in legalism) without the element of faith to direct the believer.[40] Basil demonstrated that Scripture interprets Scripture and this is accomplished by the faithful of the church and not the heresies that exist outside the church. Therefore, for Basil, faith is predicated upon biblical hermeneutics, and biblical hermeneutics is safeguarded by the faithful to preserve the Christian heritage and propagate it to the next generation.

Second Section, Part Two: Chapters 9–26

This section forms the heart of the work of On the Holy Spirit, which is the theological presentation of the biblical material discussed in the first section. Basil opened this section with Chapter 9 which serves as his introduction to the main part of the book. This chapter begins with the sanctification of the believer by the Holy Spirit. In other words, the holiness of God was ever on the mind of Basil:

> All things thirsting for holiness turn to Him; everything living
> in virtue never turns away from Him. He waters them with His

---

38. Georges Florovsky, 'The Function of Tradition in the Ancient Church,' *The Greek Orthodox Theological Review* 9:2 (1963), pp. 74-5.

39. Cyril Karam, 'Saint Basil on the Holy Spirit – Some Aspects of His Theology,' *In Honor of Saint Basil the Great* (Still River, MA: St. Bede's Publications, 1979), p. 150.

40. This line of reasoning is commanded by Jude 3, 17. Jude encourages the believer to contend for the faith that was handed down by the apostles. The issue of tradition is that it safeguards against those who are ungodly and desire to supplant the truth.

life-giving breath and helps them reach their proper fulfillment. He perfects all other things, and Himself lacks nothing; He gives life to all things, and is never depleted. He does not increase by additions, but is always complete, self-established, and present everywhere. His is the source of sanctification, spiritual light, who gives illumination to everyone using His powers to search for the truth – and the illumination He gives is Himself.[41]

The concept advocated by Basil is that the ministry of the Holy Spirit is to accomplish holiness in the believer. The rationale for this thought is that only God is Holy and since holiness is accomplished by the Holy Spirit, He must be God.

However, the focal point of this passage is placed upon the role of sanctification in the believer. Through the ministry of the Holy Spirit, in the process of sanctification, the believer encounters the Son. Basil wrote:

Only when a man has been cleansed from the shame of his evil, and has returned to his natural beauty, and the original form of the Royal Image has been restored in him, is it possible for him to approach the Paraclete. Then, like the sun, He will show you Himself in the image of the invisible, and with purified eyes you will see in this blessed image the unspeakable beauty of its prototype.[42]

Basil depicted that the Holy Spirit's ministry, in the process of sanctification, is to reveal the person of Jesus Christ to the believer (image of the invisible) and to the glory of the Father. Here, in a theologically concise statement, Basil depicted the economic Trinity as it relates to the ontological being of God.[43] The Holy Spirit sanctifies the believer while at the same time ushers the believer into the Son's presence and allows the vision of the Father to take place.

---

41. Basil, *On the Holy Spirit*, 9:22, 43.

42. Ibid., 9:23, 44.

43. This expression is almost identical to Karl Rahner's axiom, 'The "economic" Trinity is the "immanent" Trinity and the "immanent" Trinity is the "economic" Trinity.' See, Karl Rahner, *The Trinity* (New York: Crossroad Publishing, 1997), p. 22.

Economic Trinity: The word 'economic' refers to the view that the distinctions within the Trinity (differences of persons) depend upon their separate functions. These separate functions are in relation to the created universe and towards humanity. To give an example, the difference between the Son and the Holy Spirit is differentiated in their differing roles in soteriology. It is the Son who incarnated to die to secure salvation yet it is the Spirit which convicts the individual to be saved. There are two separate functions securing the Father's plan of soteriology. Thus, the economy of each Trinitarian member is the focal point of this position.

This allowed Basil to demonstrate that the Trinity is not only economic, but one. The consequence of embracing one member and rejecting another seems absurd and allows the person's faith to be questioned. Basil stated, 'If a man calls upon God, but rejects the Son, his faith is empty. If someone rejects the Spirit, his faith in the Father and the Son is made useless; it is impossible to believe in the Father and the Son without the presence of the Spirit … it is impossible to call upon the Father except in the Spirit of adoption.'[44]

Immanent Trinity: The immanent Trinity refers to the relationships of the divine persons to one another in the Trinity. The view takes the position that God is by His very nature self-communicating. One of the biblical evidences of this may be found in Genesis 1:26 where the statement is to make humanity in 'our image.' If God is self-communicating, then the immanent Trinity can only refer to Trinity communication itself, whereas, in the economic Trinity, God communicates to humanity. These two positions are not mutually exclusive but complementary.

The background of this section is built upon the baptismal formula of the triune God. The establishment of the Trinity as one is necessary so that the question is considered in terms of one Triune God at work. Thus, Matthew 28:19 becomes the focal point for worship since baptism is an act of obedience of

---

44. Basil, *On the Holy Spirit*, 11:27, 48.

the worshiper as one enters into the fellowship of both Trinity and ecclesia. Basil wrote:

> Did He[45] not clearly command His disciples to baptize all nations 'in the name of the Father, and of the Son, and of the Holy Spirit?' He did not disdain His fellowship with the Holy Spirit, but these men say that we should not rank Him with the Father and Son. Are they not openly disregarding God's commandment? ... But no one is so shameless that he will deny the obvious meaning of the words which clearly say the Spirit *is* one with the Father and the Son.[46]

The thrust of this argument is that Basil underscored the Trinitarian unity of Father, Son, and Holy Spirit working in the ecclesia. Thus, an ecclesia cannot exist without having the Holy Spirit as part of its structural foundation which, in turn, validates the church as belonging to the Triune God. In other words, it is the Holy Spirit which constitutes the church!

The Holy Spirit, in the believer, within the church

The Holy Spirit sanctifies the believer while constituting the church as the possession of the Triune God. Basil elaborated on the process in chapter 18, verse 47. He stated:

> He reveals the glory of the Only-Begotten in Himself, and He gives true worshippers the knowledge of God in Himself. The way to divine knowledge ascends from one Spirit through the one Son to the one Father. Likewise, natural goodness, inherent holiness and royal dignity reaches from the Father through the Only-Begotten to the Spirit. Thus, we do not lose the true doctrine of one God by confessing the persons.[47]

The ascendancy, or progression, of the Holy Spirit in the life of the believer is a work of Trinitarian grace. The ascendancy movement

---

45.   Reference to God added for clarity.

46.   Basil, *On the Holy Spirit*, 10:24, 45.

47.   Ibid., 18:47, 74-5.

is the work of grace, whereby, the Holy Spirit works in the internal lives of all believers, spiritually preparing their hearts for more of God. Boris Bobrinskoy stated, 'The Spirit marks the starting point of the divine work: he acts within the interior, spiritual life of human creatures, awakening them to God.'[48]

The ascendancy or progression movement is the process of sanctification of the believer in the presence of God. The believer, through the work of the Spirit, becomes sanctified in the Lord because of the Trinitarian grace bestowed upon the believer through the Spirit. The focal point is that the believer can know the Father only because of the Son and one can know the Son only through the Spirit.

The descending movement of the Holy Spirit is that He takes that which belongs to the Father, reveals it to the believer through the Son. In this way Basil used the prepositions to indicate that the static activity of the Trinity is not defined by mere words but by their mutual work of grace towards the believer within the Trinity.

Basil connected the sanctification of the believer with worship when he wrote, 'To worship in the Spirit implies that our intelligence has been enlightened.'[49] The ministry of ascending/descending is for the sanctified worship of the one triune God. This prompted Basil to state that one cannot worship God at all if one is outside the Spirit simply because God cannot be separated in worship.[50]

The Holy Spirit as person and Trinity

The principal concern for Basil was to address the doxologies in relation to the Godhead. His desire to defend his personal doxological formula revealed that he considered the Holy Spirit

48. Boris Bobrinskoy, 'The Indwelling of the Spirit in Christ: "Pneumatic Christology" in the Cappadocian Fathers,' *St. Vladimir's Theological Quarterly* 28:1 (January 1984), p. 55.

49. Basil, *On the Holy Spirit*, 26:63, 97.

50. Ibid.

to be God although he never forthrightly made that claim. For example, he never used the orthodox terminology, *homoousios*. However, Basil placed the Holy Spirit within the Trinity, which is tantamount to saying that the Holy Spirit is God.

The theological language Basil used to determine the divinity of the Holy Spirit may be termed 'a shorthand' in place of the full-blown direct language of Nicea.[51] In other words, Basil used the terminology without using the expression that has become famous, *three hypostases, one essence*. Again, in Chapter 18:44-45 he wrote that Christians 'declare each person (*hypostases*)' and Christians confess the 'uniqueness of the persons (*hypostases*)'. The meaning is that *hypostases* refers to the persons involved within the Trinity. Basil declared that each member of the Trinity is its own person. By doing so, he avoided the common mistake of associating *hypostases* with *ousia* (essence).

This use of language has the direct meaning that whatever is common to the Godhead is deemed *ousia* and what is characteristic to each individual is termed *hypostases*. Therefore, in shorthand, Basil gave the Trinitarian formula of one *ousia* (essence or substance as related to a living being), three *hypostases* (persons as related to distinct persons and personalities). The objection to Basil's Trinitarian formula is that it may allow for Tri-theism or subordinationism. Basil, anticipating this objection, maintained the unity of the Monarchy or the Fatherhood of God. Again, he wrote, 'The Son is in the Father and the Father in the Son; what the Father is the Son is, the Son is likewise and vice versa – such is unity.'[52] Concerning the possible charge of subordinationism, Basil countered, 'Those who teach subordination, and talk about first, second, and third, ought to realize that they are introducing erroneous Greek polytheism into pure Christian theology.'[53]

---

51.   Behr, *The Nicene Faith*, vol. 2, part 2, p. 308.

52.   Basil, *On the Holy Spirit*, 18:45, 72.

53.   Ibid., 18:47, 75.

Legacy of 'On the Holy Spirit'

There is no doubt that Basil was the first to speak of God in terms that clarified His existence. Robert Letham stated that Basil's work, *On the Holy Spirit*, was the 'first recorded instance of Basil using *hypostases* to denote that God is three, thereby opening the way to speak of the Trinity in clearer language.'[54] Bobrinskoy continued his praise of Basil as he wrote:

> The great theological innovation of St. Basil will be to determine the theological distinction between essence (ousia) and the Persons (*hypostases*) and to bring out the characteristics of the specific and inalienable hypostatic attributes of each person. That is, with the help of biblical revelation, he tried to define the unique character of each divine Person, in the work of creation and salvation, on the one hand, and, starting from there, also in the eternal relations of the Trinitarian Persons ... The distinction between the essence and the *hypostases* worked out by St. Basil constitutes from then on a definitive asset for Orthodox Trinitarian doctrine, an asset which his companions in arms would faithfully take over.[55]

Bobrinskoy recognized that Basil's contribution to pneumatology and Trinitarian studies was substantial. Basil's work contributed to the demise of the semi-Arians and became the standard for Trinitarian studies for the next one thousand years in Christianity.

Council of Constantinople

Basil died 1 January 379 and, therefore, never witnessed his contribution to the issue of the Trinity. The Empire's political scene changed as Emperor Valens died, which left the Arians without imperial support. The new Emperor, Theodosius, called a council at Constantinople in early summer 381, two years after the death of Basil. This council issued four canons which declared the boundaries of orthodox doctrine concerning the Trinity.

---

54. Letham, *The Holy Trinity*, p. 149.

55. Bobrinskoy, *The Mystery of the Trinity*, pp. 233-4.

The first reaffirmed the Nicene Creed and anathematized the errors which had arisen since 325. Thus, the Eunomians, the Arians, the Pneumatomachians, and the Marcillians, all were deemed heretical. The second canon restricted the activity of each bishop to his local See. The third canon declared the Bishop of Constantinople to have the same prerogatives as the Bishop of Rome, since the city of Constantinople was the new headquarters of the Roman Empire. The fourth canon declared the ministry of Maximus the Cynic as invalid.[56]

The council also produced the most significant document since 325, the Creed of Constantinople. The third article of the creed reads, 'We believe in the Holy Spirit, the Lord, the giver of Life, who proceeds from the Father. With the Father and Son he is worshipped and glorified.'[57] The statement settled the issue of Arianism as a force within the church in the eastern portion of the Empire. This council ratified the position that the Holy Spirit was consubstantial with the Father and the Son.

Two other items are noteworthy of mention. The council also produced a list of bishops who were deemed orthodox in the churches. Two men in particular stand out: one is the brother of Basil, Gregory of Nyssa. In all likelihood it was Gregory's influence that helped produce the creed which so resembles his brother's work. The second person of note is the young man whom Basil responded to in his work, On the Holy Spirit (i.e., the young disciple of Basil, Amphilochius of Iconium).[58] Perhaps, the work of On the Holy Spirit not only established the orthodox position of the Trinity, but also may

---

56. Behr, The Nicene Faith, vol. 2, part 1, p. 121. However, Philip Schaff stated that there were seven canons produced. See, Schaff, History of the Christian Church, vol. 3, p. 640.

57. 'The Constantinople Creed of 381' in The Creeds of Christendom, vol. 1, ed. Philip Schaff (Grand Rapids, MI: Baker Books House, 1998), p. 29.

58. Theodoret, 'The Ecclesiastical History,' in Nicene and Post-Nicene Fathers, 2nd Series, eds. Philip Schaff and Henry Wace, vol. 3 (Peabody, MA: Hendrickson Publishers, 1994), p. 136.

have directed a young pastor into the truth of God to help serve the people of God.

The second item that should be recognized is that the Constantinople Creed of 381 became the universal creed of the east and eventually in the west. Letham stated:

> Since its origin, over fifty generations of the church in both East and West have confessed their faith using its words ... The Protestant Reformers asserted the supreme authority of Holy Scripture, but the Reformers to a man wanted to keep this creed, for they respected the historic teaching of the church and accorded it an authority of its own.[59]

Creeds are only as good as the integrity of men who wish to keep them. However, the fact that the Council of Constantinople, fifty generations of Christians, and the Protestant Reformers all sought to keep this creed, reflects the truth of God as found in the Scriptures. Well done, Basil!

---

59. Letham, *The Holy Trinity*, p. 181.

6

BASIL'S *HEXAEMERON*

In the year A.D. 378, during Lent, Basil preached a series entitled *Hexaemeron.*[1] The title *Hexaemeron* refers to 'the account of creation of the universe in six days, as set forth in Genesis One.'[2] Thus, Basil preached nine sermons on the topic of the six days of creation. As one can surmise from the title, the hermeneutical approach to reading Genesis, for Basil, was literal. He used the literal hermeneutic which arrives at the conclusion that everything revealed in Genesis is factual. Therefore, this work is one of the earliest works on Genesis that argues for six literal days for the creation of the world. Certainly, it is one of the most well-known works of the early Church Fathers that depict creation taking place as six literal days.

Basil's rationale for utilizing the literal hermeneutic

Basil was well acquainted with the allegorical method of interpretation. During his monastic years, he translated Origen's *Philocalia.*[3] Richard Lim commented, 'The first section of the *Philocalia* is dedicated to Origen's exegetical principles. The selection is concerned

1. Saint Basil, *Exegetical Homilies*, trans., Agnes Clare Way, *Fathers of the Church* 46 (Washington, D.C.: Catholic University of America Press, 1963).

2. F. L. Cross and E. A. Livingstone (eds.), *The Oxford Dictionary of the Christian Church*, 3rd ed. (Oxford: Oxford University Press, 1997), s.v. '*Hexaemeron*' p. 765.

3. See Chapter Two.

with the divine inspiration of scriptures, the problem of biblical languages and stresses the importance of spiritual exegesis.'[4]

Basil was familiar with the allegorical or spiritualizing hermeneutic as he often used it in his own work. For example, Basil also preached a series on the Psalms where he employed the allegorizing hermeneutic.[5] What is most interesting is that he preached these sermons in close proximity to the date of the sermons of the *Hexaemeron*. Working with Fedwick's dates, the Homily on Psalm 33 was preached during 373, the Homily on Psalm 28 during 374, and the Homily on Psalms 32 and 45 during 375.[6]

> **Allegorical hermeneutic:** The allegorical hermeneutic is predicated upon the word 'allegory,' the means of which is to 'speak one way and signifying or meaning another from that which is said.' The use of allegory was acceptable in the early church in order to reveal a deeper spiritual truth. For example, Moses crossing the Red Sea was often understood to be a reference to baptism in the New Testament understanding. Origen is regarded as the leading proponent of the allegorical hermeneutic. The Alexandrian School followed Origen and taught this particular method of interpretation.

One example of Basil's allegorical interpretation will suffice. In Psalm 28, Basil referred to the ram as an animal that is capable of leadership. He connected the meaning of the ram's leadership to those who are pastors or leaders of congregations. He wrote, 'Such are those who are set over the flock of Christ, since they lead them forth to the flowery and fragrant nourishment of spiritual doctrine.'[7] The Psalm passage

---

4. Richard Lim, 'The Politics of Interpretation in Basil of Caesarea's *Hexaemeron*,' *Vigiliae Christianae* 44 (1990), p. 351.

5. Saint Basil, *Exegetical Homilies*. Both sermon series, the *Hexaemeron* and the Psalms are recorded in the same book by Agnes Clare Way.

6. Paul Jonathan Fedwick, 'Appendix A' in *The Church and the Charisma of Leadership in Basil of Caesarea* (Toronto: Pontifical Institute of Medieval Studies, 1979), pp. 145-52.

7. Saint Basil, 'Homily 13 on Psalms 28,' in *Exegetical Homilies*, trans., Agnes Clare Way, *Fathers of the Church* 46 (Washington, D.C.: Catholic University of America Press, 1963), p. 195.

refs to David completing the Tabernacle and worshiping God.[8] The focus upon the ram is an act of worship but Basil wrote his sermon in such a way that the ram was the focal point for leading others to worship. Thus, Basil understood that Psalm 28 speaks of pastoral ministry.

Allegory versus literal

The natural question that arises is, 'Did Basil abandon the *allegorical* hermeneutic at the end of his ministry in favor of the *literal* hermeneutic?' The answer is not as easily given as the question presupposes. The most-used hermeneutic was Origen's threefold application, where the exegete utilized: (1) the literal sense to determine the meaning of the words, (2) the spiritual sense to determine the application of the words, and (3) the allegorical sense to help the mind embrace the spiritual truths contained in the words.[9] Although Origen affirmed the literal interpretation of the Scriptures, he thought and taught that the primary sense of interpretation belonged to the spiritual sense. Kelly affirmed that Origen preferred the spiritual sense of interpretation as he stated, 'Origen's three senses of Scripture, deeming that recourse to the spiritual meaning was made necessary by the anthropomorphisms, inconsistencies, and incongruities in which the Bible abounded.'[10]

Literal hermeneutic: The literal hermeneutic takes the position that the text has a concrete meaning. Thus, the intended meaning of the author is pivotal to understanding the meaning of Scripture. In the patristic era, the meaning of *litera* was underscored by the premise that the Scriptures originated from God in a supernatural way which did not allow for a neutral meaning devoid of faith. For the patristic exegete, the practice of the literal method of interpretation was also a spiritual exercise. This particular position was followed by the School of Antioch.

8.   The actual Psalm 28 in Basil's day was Psalm 29 in modern versions of the Bible.

9.   David Dockery, *Christian Perspective: An Evangelical Perspective on Inspiration, Authority and Interpretation* (Nashville, TN: Broadman and Holman Publishers, 1995), p. 110.

10. Kelly, *Early Christian Doctrines*, p. 75.

Basil was highly aware and very much utilized the allegorical method of interpretation, except in the *Hexaemeron*. Therefore, again he does not use this hermeneutical method in his sermons on Genesis but does so in the Psalms. Before an adequate answer can be given to the question of whether Basil abandoned the allegorical hermeneutic at the end of his ministry in favor of the literal reading, a review of the *Hexaemeron* contents concerning allegory must be considered.

The witness of the *Hexaemeron*

Basil denounced the allegorical method of interpretation in three places within the *Hexaemeron*. In Homily 2:4, Basil addressed the issue of myths and interpretation. He stated:

> 'And darkness,' Moses said, 'was on the face of the deep.' Here, again, are other opportunities for myths and sources for more impious fabrications, since men pervert the words according to their own notions. They explain the darkness, not as some unlighted air, as is natural, or a place over-shadowed by the interposition of a body, or, in short, a place deprived of light through any cause whatsoever, but, they explain the darkness as evil power, or rather, as evil itself, having it beginning from itself, resisting and opposing the goodness of God ... From this beginning, then, what wicked of godless dogmas have not been invented![11]

Basil did not address the interpreters he was accusing of making myths as he only referred to them as *they*. He did address the result of their interpretation. He stated that their explanation of darkness referred to evil powers and stated that this interpretation comes at the expense of a more natural reading. Interestingly, he calls these myths inventions. Basil's meaning could not be more pointed. To embrace a myth is to denounce the plain reading of the Scriptures.

11. Saint Basil, 'Homily 2 of The *Hexaemeron*' in *Exegetical Homilies*, trans., Agnes Clare Way, *Fathers of the Church* 46 (Washington, D.C.: Catholic University of America Press, 1963), p. 26.

The second time Basil addressed the allegorical method was in Homily 3, commenting on the division of the waters in Genesis 1. In this sermon, he wrote against those who interpret Genesis with a spiritual sense:

> We have also some argument concerning the division of the waters with those writers of the Church who, on a pretext of the spiritual sense and of more sublime concepts, have recourse to allegories, saying that spiritual and incorporeal powers are signified figuratively by the waters, that the more excellent have remained up above the firmament, but the malignant remain below in the terrestrial and material regions.[12]

This statement was directed against the writers or interpreters within the church who used the spiritual sense of interpretation to conclude a meaning that is unintended by the Scriptures. Basil proved his point by referencing Daniel's revelation of the three Hebrew children who escaped the fire of Nebuchadnezzar (see Ps. 148). The poignant story of Meshach, Shadrach, and Abednego demonstrates that the elements of the world are called upon to the praise the Lord. The meaning is that the division of waters does not represent evil powers below or higher powers above. They simply are created waters that heed the command of the Lord.

Basil's most prolific criticism of the allegory interpretation is found in Homily 9:1. He compared his approach to the literal interpretation of Elijah and being a good host, even though the food consisted of vegetables rather than meat. The meaning of this comparison is that Basil must have received some mild criticism for his sermon as he did not use the allegorical method. The comparison of food being consumed by Elijah's guest, and the sermon preached by Basil, underscores the fact that his desire for the congregants is to consume the sumptuous food of his sermon.[13] Basil assured his readers of the following:

---

12. Saint Basil, 'Homily 3 of The *Hexaemeron*,' pp. 51-2.

13. Saint Basil, 'Homily 9 of The *Hexaemeron*,' p. 135.

I know the laws of allegory, although I did not invent them of myself, but have met them in the works of others. Those who do not admit the common meaning of Scriptures say that water is not water, but some other nature, and they explain a plant and a fish according to their opinion. They describe also the production of reptiles and wild animals, changing it according to their own notions, just like the dream interpreters, who interpret for their own ends the appearances seen in their dreams.[14]

Basil pointedly stated that he knew how to interpret allegory but chose the literal method. He compared the allegorical method to people who reads dreams for their own personal agenda. In the mind of Basil, this did not profit those who desire understanding from God's Word.

In a unique but not unmitigated turn, Basil connected the literal method of interpretation to the gospel message. He stated, 'When I hear grass, I think of grass, and in the same manner I understand everything as it is said, a plant, a fish, a wild animal, and an ox. Indeed I am not ashamed of the gospel.'[15] The relationship between the gospel, Genesis, and the literal method of interpretation is the presentation of the clear and forthright message that is yielded by the literal method. This is in stark contrast to the allegorical method which does not allow for a clear presentation of the text. The allegorical method, according to Basil, only distorts the meaning of the Scriptures. He wrote:

This is a thing of which they seem to me to have been unaware, who have attempted by false arguments and allegorical interpretations to bestow on the Scripture a dignity of their own meaning. But, theirs is the attitude of one who considers himself wiser than the revelations of the Spirit and introduces his own ideas in pretense of an explanation. Therefore, let it be understood at it was written.[16]

---

14. Saint Basil, Homily 9, p. 135

15. Ibid.

16. Ibid., p. 136.

Three times in this sermon series Basil denounced the allegorical hermeneutic, basing that decision upon the fact that the allegorist presumes to have more knowledge than the Scriptures. Basil certainly was aware of Aristotle's, *On the Heavens*, and his *Metaphysics*, but these works do not seem to be the object of his refutation in the *Hexaemeron*. He declared that those who were in the church using the allegorical method were the focus of his refutation. Therefore, since he was preaching to the church certainly his desire was for the congregants to hear the story of creation without the fanciful interpretations, myths, and personal agendas that the allegories lend themselves.

One certainly can conclude accurately that Basil did not use the allegorical method for Genesis, but that does not mean he totally rejected it necessarily. Gregory of Nazianzen alluded to the fact that Basil used allegory for the edification of the soul. He stated:

> His other treatises, in which he gives explanations for those who are shortsighted, by a threefold inscription on the solid tablets of his heart, lead me on from mere literal or symbolical interpretation to a still wider view, as I proceed from one depth to another, calling upon deep after deep, and finding light after light, until I attain the highest pinnacle.[17]

The question, 'Did Basil abandon the allegorical hermeneutic at the end of his ministry in favour of the literal hermeneutic?' can be answered in this way: he did abandon that particular hermeneutic as viable for the interpretation for Genesis. That does not mean he denounced the use of it permanently. He did recognize the misuse of allegory where it contradicts the text. Basil's purpose, as stated by Gregory, was to lead the reader or hearer to a greater knowledge of God's truth in the Word.

Therefore, Basil used allegory for his sermons on Psalms. In addition, Gregory of Nazianzen acknowledged that Basil also

---

17. Gregory of Nazianzen, *The Panegyric on St. Basil*, p. 418.

used it consistently throughout his works so that one could learn deep truths of the Lord. However, the following question must be raised: Why did he abandon the use of allegory for the *Hexaemeron*? This question becomes relevant in light of the above conclusion that Basil sought to lead his congregants into truth.

Richard Lim's theory

Richard Lim, in an article, has provided a thought-provoking discussion as to the reason Basil chose to interpret the *Hexaemeron* literally. Lim proposed, 'Basil was leading his humble congregation by the hand in a gradual anagogy [spiritual interpretation], using the literalist hermeneutics which he considered to be most appropriate to his audience.'[18] Since the *Hexaemeron* was a series of sermons preached at Lent, it is reasonable to assume that not only was the congregation present but perhaps people also were present who had not been associated specifically with the church permanently.

Lim demonstrated that the *Hexaemeron* revealed the social structure of some of the people associated with the audience at Caesarea. Lim – alluding to *Hexaemeron* Homily 3.1 – stated, 'Basil acknowledges the presence of a group of tradesmen who apparently took the day off to hear him preach.'[19] In order to evaluate Lim's proposal, a review of Homily 3.1 is necessary. Basil acknowledged, 'It has not escaped my notice, however, that many workers of handicrafts, who with difficulty provide a livelihood for themselves from their daily toil, are gathered around us. These compel us to cut short our discourse in order that they may not be drawn away too long from their work.'[20]

Basil was concerned that the worker must not be too long from his labor. So as to ensure the secure employment of his congregants, therefore, Basil did not speak too long during the sermons. This

---

18. Richard Lim, 'The Politics of Interpretation in Basil of Caesarea's *Hexaemeron*,' p. 352.

19. Lim, 'The Politics of Interpretation,' p. 361.

20. Saint Basil, 'Homily 3 of The *Hexaemeron*,' p. 37.

strongly implies that his audiences during Lent were workers who must give the employer a full day's labor for the wage received. Paul Fedwick confirmed the social structure of the audience as he stated, 'The hearers of Basil's homilies belonged to varied classes and occupations, with the poor class predominating.'[21]

A second passage that Lim used to solidify his thesis is Homily 7:5-7 of the *Hexaemeron*. Lim took the position that Basil knew his audience as being husbands who were rough and inhumane. Lim noted, 'Some he accuses of being libertines and inhumane husbands.'[22] Lim is not without warrant but the accusation may be harsh in view of Basil's comments. Basil, quoting Ephesians 5:25, encouraged each husband to love his wife as they are united in marriage. He illustrated that the viper, regardless of being a cruel animal, marries and embraces the union. Then, he pointedly made the application. Basil stated, 'What do my words mean? That, even if the husband is rough, even if he is fierce in his manners, the wife must endure and for no cause whatsoever permit herself to break the union.'[23]

There is no doubt that the congregation demographics were of the lower social structure. However, Lim's argument that Basil made an accusation is unwarranted. The evidence suggested that the husbands needed to learn refinement in order to love the wife. However, to make the case of husbands acting inhumanely seems unreasonable, although the main point is well taken. The audience did not have the sophisticated expertise to listen to an allegorical sermon.

The final passage that Lim used is Homily 8 of the *Hexaemeron*. Lim interpreted this passage to mean that Basil's audience preferred vice over virtue. Lim wrote that Basil 'openly professes to be afraid that once he dismisses his congregation, some

21. Paul Jonathan Fedwick, *The Church and the Charisma of Leadership in Basil of Caesarea*, p. 6.

22. Richard Lim, 'The Politics of Interpretation in Basil of Caesarea's *Hexaemeron*,' p. 361.

23. Saint Basil, 'Homily 7 of The *Hexaemeron*,' p. 114.

of them would rush to the dice.'[24] Lim's insight was taken from a direct quote of Basil concerning his congregation. Basil wrote:

> If I shall dismiss you and put an end to the assembly, there are some who will run to the gaming tables. Their oaths and cruel contentions and pangs of avarice are to be found. The demon stands by, inflaming the passions, with dotted bones and changing the same money from one side of the table to the other, now leading this one on by victory and throwing that one into despair; again, causing the first to bear himself proudly and the latter to be covered with shame ... Perhaps, some profit will be found in what I have said; but, if not, at least, because you have been kept occupied here, you have not sinned. Therefore, to detain you longer is to withdraw you for a longer time from evils.[25]

Basil acknowledged that his congregants were drawn to the seedier side of life. However, he did not despair over the condition of his congregation but simply encouraged them in their relationship with the Lord.

Lim does seem to be correct in his analysis of Basil's congregation at Caesarea. The fact is that the literal method speaks to the common meaning of Scripture so that the average church member would comprehend the meaning of the text. On the other hand, the allegorical method would lend itself to fanciful interpretations among those who heard it. Basil's fear about using the allegorical approach seemed to be that his audience would be led to heresy. In order to safeguard his congregation, the wise pastor Basil did not use an interpretive method that would allow 'heretical predators' to corrupt the listener's heart by corrupting the Word.[26] Lim praised Basil's pastoral abilities when he stated, 'The Shepherd is capable of protecting his flock as long as the sheep do not stray too far on their own.'[27]

---

24. Richard Lim, 'The Politics of Interpretation in Basil of Caesarea's *Hexaemeron*,' p. 361.

25. Saint Basil, 'Homily 8 of The *Hexaemeron*,' p. 133.

26. Richard Lim, 'The Politics of Interpretation in Basil of Caesarea's *Hexaemeron*,', p. 363.

27. Ibid.

Richard Lim correctly identified the rationale of Basil. His concern for his congregation meant that Basil limited himself to preaching to them for the better understanding of the Word. The best way to accomplish this was to avoid allegorical methodology which led to heresy. Thus, his sermons on the *Hexaemeron* are a treasured tool not only for their content but for their attitude of service to the people of God.

The Content of the *Hexaemeron*

Basil's purpose is to reveal the cosmology of Genesis. However, the sermons do not reveal that the cosmology stands sufficiently as the focal point of God's creation. The account of humanity's creation within the cosmology, and the ultimate concept of humanity's destiny within the cosmology, is the central theme that occupies Basil's theme. Rousseau further advocated that Basil sought to demonstrate that humanity would return to the Fatherland, which was his metaphor for returning 'to a world that was invisible and eternal.'[28]

Since the Christian account of cosmology is profiled highly, it should be expected that the sermons also are focused upon the salvation of humanity. The response of salvation is not just the issue of a new created order, although that is key to Basil's thought. The *Hexaemeron* demonstrated that salvation was always the primary goal of the Father, which is the promise of the New Testament. Thus, the objective reality of the cosmos and salvation of humanity were bound together inextricably in that renewal was not only cosmological but soteriological. For this reason, Basil denounced the wisdom of the world as incapable of containing the truth of God. Basil noted, 'Let us hear, therefore, the words of truth expressed not in the persuasive language of human wisdom, but in the teachings of the Spirit, whose end is not praise from those hearing, but the salvation of those

28. Rousseau, *Basil of Caesarea*, p. 320.

taught.'[29] Building upon the soteriological aspects of humanity within the cosmos, Basil used the *Hexaemeron* to establish the fundamental difference between the world views of his day (i.e., a contrast between Christian and pagan accounts) for the creation of the world.

The sovereignty of God

Basil stressed that there was a single explanation for the existence of the cosmos. He perpetuated the theological premise that God is creator of the cosmos and is in control of His creation. The fact that God is in control of the cosmos rules out fatalism as a guiding factor for the destiny of cosmology. Basil emphatically stated this point several times in the *Hexaemeron*. A review of three different Homilies within the series will suffice to prove the point. In Homily 5:8, after reviewing the growth process of the plants, he stated, 'Nothing happens without cause; nothing by chance; all things involve a certain ineffable wisdom.'[30] The ineffable wisdom is not the cosmos itself but the Creator of the cosmos that established the patterns of growth for the plants.

> **Fatalism:** The pagan world view that adheres to the position that all things are determined by blind, irrational forces and human effort cannot change the events or outcomes. The predisposed outcomes mean that humanity is trapped in a world that he cannot change. Humanity is a victim (pro or con) of blind irrationality and has no choice but to accept its fate.

Homily 7:5 also records Basil's concept of God's sovereignty. Basil referred to the fish as understanding its own environment. In the same way that sailors understand their environment as they traverse the seas, he demonstrated that astronomers understand barometric pressure which is germane to their field of study. However, Basil did not attribute this understanding to the intelligence

29. Saint Basil, 'Homily 1 of The *Hexaemeron*,' p. 4.

30. Saint Basil, Homily 5:8, 79.

of the plant, animal, or human. He gave credit to God for the creature's ability to relate to the cosmos. Basil stated, 'There is nothing unpremeditated, nothing neglected by God. His sleeping eye beholds all things. He is present to all, providing means of preservation for each. If God has not put the sea urchin outside of His watchful care, does He not have regard for your affairs?'[31]

Basil adequately depicted that all of the affairs of humanity within the cosmos are under the watchful care of a sovereign God who loves His creation. This, of course, is what rules out fatalism within the affairs of humanity. The cosmos and all that it contains are guided by the wisdom and faithfulness of a loving Father who is worthy of praise. Basil considered this theme in Homily 8:7. He wrote:

> Everything, which by the command of God was brought forth from nonexistence into existence, and whatever my discourse has omitted at the present time so as to avoid a longer delay on these matters and so that it might not seem to extend beyond measure, may you who are studious review by yourselves, learning the wisdom of God in all things, and may you never cease from admiration nor from giving glory to the Creator for every creature.[32]

Basil affirmed that God's wisdom to create the world also demands the response of praise from those who understand His wisdom. Therefore, it is His wisdom that denounces fatalism as an explanation for the culmination or destiny of the cosmos.

The cosmos is not fatalistic as God is in control of the world and world events. The cosmos is not eternal nor was it created over time. Rather, it exists under the control of God who created the cosmos in six literal days.

Six literal days for creation

Basil affirmed the meaning of *day* in reference to creation as a twenty-four-hour period. He wrote:

31.　Saint Basil, Homily 7:5, 114.

32.　Ibid., Homily 8:7, 129.

'And there was evening and morning, one day.' Why did he say 'one' and not 'first?' And yet, it is more consistent for him who intends to introduce a second and a third and a fourth day, to call the one which begins the series 'first.' But, he said 'one' because he was defining the measure of a day and night and combining the time of a night and day, since the twenty-four hours fill up the interval of one day, if, of course, night is understood with day...It is as if one would say that the measure of twenty-four hours is the length of one day.[33]

He built this argument on the fact that the word *day* specifies a twenty-four-hour time unit to regulate the measurement of time on earth. Basil continued:

So that, as often as through the revolution of the sun evening and morning traverse the world, the circle is completed, not in a longer period of time, but in the space of one day ... That God having prepared the nature of time, set as measures and limits for it the intervals of the days, and measuring it out for a week, He ordered the week, in counting the change of time, always to return again in a circle to itself. Again, He orders that one day by recurring seven times complete a week; and this, beginning from itself and ending on itself, is the form of a circle.[34]

Basil understood that temporal time also was created in order to regulate the sequence of time. The cycle of a week is predicated upon a literal twenty-four-hour period which sustains creation. The fact is hard to miss. If time is created in increments of twenty-four hours, and since seven twenty-four-hour periods comprise a week, then creation itself must have been created and sustained within the same time frame.

Yet time is not the purpose for all of creation. Basil related time to eternity and built his case that the twenty-four-hour periods of literal succession of time are a preview of eschatology. He stated:

33. Saint Basil, Homily 2:8, 34.
34. Ibid.

Therefore, he called the beginning of time not a 'first day,' but 'one day,' in order from the name it might have kinship with eternity. For the day which shows a character of uniqueness and non-participation with the rest is properly and naturally called 'one'... In order, therefore, to lead our thoughts to future life, he called that day 'one' which is an image of eternity, the beginning of days, the contemporary of light, the holy Lord's day, the day honored by the Resurrection of the Lord.[35]

Basil underscored that the eschatology of the cosmos is bound extricably to the timetable of the Lord's resurrection. Therefore, the intervals of time on earth that witnessed that event are not *ages upon ages*, but a set time within the framework of creation. Since the Lord's life was lived in the interval of time as expressed in a twenty-four-hour day, Basil linked the resurrection to the creation of time within twenty-four-hour periods. Thus, Basil concluded that creation, the Lord's life and death, His resurrection, the worship of the Lord, and indeed eschatology as a whole, are bound to the cosmos which was created in twenty-four literal hours.

The particular phases of the Lord's life that Basil recalled are bound in time and, thus, are subject to the created elements of a twenty-four-hour period. There is no discontinuity of time for Basil in creation. In other words, time as expressed in creation in a twenty-four-hour period, is also time expressed that contains and sustains creation within the same twenty-four hour-period.

Creation instantaneous and *ex nihilo*

The prevailing thought of the fourth century concerning *matter* was that it was eternal. Plato's account of the cosmos was popular in the fourth century. According to Plato, *matter* always existed and the creation of the cosmos was from matter that existed in an unformed state prior to the creation. Norman Geisler noted, 'Plato believed the universe is eternal, an eternal process by

---

35.   Saint Basil, Homily 2:8, 35.

which the Creator (*Demiuergos*) beheld the Good (the *Agathos*) and overflowed with Forms (*Eidos*) which informed the material world (Chaos) forever, forming it into a cosmos. Creation, then, is an eternal process of ex material creation.'[36]

Basil denounced Platonic thought with the expression 'in the beginning' (*evn vrch/*). The concept of 'beginning' means that the cosmos had a starting point found in God and therefore, it is not eternal. Since the cosmos has a starting point, the cause of such beginning (*evn avrch/*) is God. This argument denounces pre-existing eternal matter as being used of God to construct the cosmos. Basil wrote, 'Or, perhaps, the words, "in the beginning he created," were used because of the instantaneous and timeless act of creation, since the beginning is something immeasurable and indivisible.'[37]

Basil argued for the instantaneous creation of the cosmos which countered the prevailing thought of the contemporary fourth-century pagan account that the cosmos is eternal. He addressed these pagan accounts as he wrote:

> The wise Moses used no other word concerning it, but he said: 'in the beginning he created.' He did not say: 'He produced,' nor 'He fashioned,' but 'he created.' Inasmuch as many of those who imagined that the world from eternity co-existed with God did not concede that it was made by Him, but that, being, as it were, a shadow of His power, it existed of itself coordinately with Him, and inasmuch as they admit that God is the cause of it, but involuntarily a cause, as the body is the cause of the shadow and the flashing light the cause of the brilliance, therefore, the prophet in correcting such an error uses exactness in his words, saying: 'in the beginning God created.'[38]

Basil placed the authority of the Scripture above the prevailing notions of philosophy and science. His argument was on the

---

36. Norman Geisler, *Baker Encyclopedia of Christian Apologetics* (Grand Rapids, MI: Baker Academic, 2007), s.v. 'Plato.'

37. Saint Basil, 'Homily 1:6 of The *Hexaemeron*,' p. 11.

38. Ibid., p. 12.

minute definition of the words 'beginning' and 'created.' J. C. M. VanWinden observed, 'The term beginning is not an indication of time but of the indivisible moment of the origin of things.'[39] According to Basil, there can be no beginning of the cosmos prior to God's act of creation. The creation of the cosmos *ex nihilo* means that God created without pre-existing *matter*.

ex nihilo: A Latin phrase meaning 'out of nothing.' It is used to depict that God created the universe out of nothing or, in other words, there was no pre-existing matter utilized for creation, as it did not exist. Creation came into being as a result of God's own creative power and energy.

Young earth and evolution

Basil did not argue for the age of the earth specifically. However, at the risk of being anachronistic, Basil inadvertently addressed the issue of the earth or the theory of evolution when he argued that 'in the beginning' (*evn avrch/*) is connected to the literal meaning of the word *day*. Basil argued that if age were meant instead of a literal twenty-four-hour time period, Moses would have used the phrase as found elsewhere in the Scripture. He wrote:

> If, however, the Scripture presents to us many ages, saying in various places, 'age of age,' and 'ages to ages,' still in those places neither the first, nor the second, nor the third age is enumerated for us, so that, by this, difference of conditions and of various circumstances are shown to us but not limits and boundaries and successions of ages.[40]

Basil argued that the word 'ages' and 'day' have two distinct meanings and are nuanced by the text. Since Genesis does not reference those conditions for a specific definition then, twenty-four hours must be the meaning for creation. Taking that concept to its logical conclusion, then earth created in six literal days means that the earth

---

39. J. C. M VanWinden, 'In the Beginning: Some Observations of the Patristic Interpretation of *Genesis 1:1*,' *Vigiliae Christianae* 17 (1963), p. 110.

40. Saint Basil, 'Homily 2:8 of The *Hexaemeron*,' p. 35.

is young. This denies not only the fourth-century thought of an eternal earth, but also denounces the view that the earth is billions of years old. In fact, Basil addressed the order of years as being literal and places the creation of sun and moon as being the focal point for yearly calculation.[41]

Since Basil implied a young earth, this argument denied any possibility of an evolutionary theory that would argue for the adaptation or mutation of species. Homily 9:2 stated:

'Let the earth bring forth living creatures; cattle and wild beasts and crawling creatures.' Consider the word of God moving through all creation, having begun at that time, active up to the present, and efficacious until the end, even to the consummation of the world. As a ball, when pushed by someone and then meeting a slope, is borne downward by its own shape and the inclination of the ground and does not stop before some level surface receives it, so, too, the nature of existing objects, set in motion by one command, passes through creation, without change, by generation and destruction, preserving the succession of the species through resemblance, until it reaches the very end.[42]

Basil argued that the species were created by the Lord and then commanded to reproduce. This command still is in force for the cosmos (and its species) and will always be so. The reproduction of any species is inherent to its own creation which is subject to the command of God to reproduce. Basil did not find any evidence where creation is given another command to adapt or mutate but only to reproduce as it is the nature of itself. Again, Basil wrote:

It begets a horse as the successor of a horse, a lion of a lion, and an eagle of an eagle; and it continues to preserve each of the animals by uninterrupted successions until the consummation of the universe. No length of time causes the specific characteristics of animals to be corrupted or extinct, but, as if established just recently, nature, ever fresh, moves along with time.[43]

---

41. Saint Basil, Homily 6:8, 97.

42. Ibid., 9:2, 136-7.

43. Saint Basil, Homily 9:2, 137.

For Basil, the idea of mutation, adaptation, or evolving is not characteristic of creation. The command to reproduce is not interrupted by time that may change or corrupt the species. The opposite position is asserted. Creation moves successively with time and not counter to it, nor is creation changed by time but functions within time until time is consumed.

Contribution of the *Hexaemeron*

Basil, along with Ambrose, is one of the few early Church Fathers who contributed to a distinctly Christian world view concerning the origins of the cosmology. What is remarkable is that Basil's work was written in the Greek language, whereas Ambrose's was written in Latin, leaving speculation that Ambrose is indebted heavily to Basil. VanWinden determined, 'In conclusion, St. Ambrose is largely dependent on St. Basil.'[44]

There is also speculation that Eustathius' translation of Basil's *Hexaemeron* into Latin was the basis of Augustine's work, *The Literal Meaning of Genesis*.[45] John Callahan made this speculation as he wrote, 'It has been known for a long time that Augustine must have known Basil's work on the six days of creation, the Hexaemeron, and it has been stated in recent years that he knew this work through the Latin translation of Eustathius.'[46] Callahan cited S. Giet as a reference for this information but did not make a hard-and fast-conclusion.[47]

Regardless of influence upon later writers, Basil addressed the cosmology of his day and denounced it with solid Scriptural

44. VanWinden, 'In the Beginning: Some Observations of the Patristic Interpretation of *Genesis 1:1*,' *Vigiliae Christianae* 17 (1963), p. 121.

45. Augustine, *The Literal Meaning of Genesis*, eds., Johannes Quasten, Walter J. Burghardt, Thomas Comerford Lawler, Ancient Christian Writers, vols. 41-2 (New York, NY: Paulist Press, 1982).

46. John F. Callahan, 'Basil of Caesarea: A New Source for St. Augustine's Theory of Time,' *Harvard Studies in Classical Philology* 63 (1958), p. 440.

47. S. Giet, *Basile de Césarée, Homélies sur L'Hexaméron* (Paris, 1950), p. 7. Because of the author's deficency in French and the unavailability of the source, this work could not be validated.

arguments. He accomplished this by understanding the audience to whom he engaged during Lent in 378. This understanding allowed Basil to leave a strong legacy of six literal days of creation when most of his contemporaries were using an allegorical method. Thus, the legacy of the church has an example of a man who understood his congregants, knew how to reach them with the truth of Genesis, and, on a larger scale, left the church with the lasting legacy of reading the Bible literally even when it seems most unpopular.

Contribution to Evangelicalism

Basil contributed to modern Evangelicalism by way of example. First, he demonstrated his knowledge of the contemporary world of fourth-century science. He knew that Plato, Aristotle, and others shaped the thought of his world. His goal was to confront the common accounts of creation and address them with a biblical world view grounded in the Scriptures. This led him to grasp the meaning of Genesis with a profound understanding that the cosmos is bound to the soteriology and eschatology of the Father. For Basil, the creation of the world was not an end of itself, but the very means to the Lord's purposeful end. Thus, he understood that the Lord created with the end in mind.

Second, he placed a strong emphasis on the sovereignty of God to guide His creation to its intended end. The result is that fatalism is denounced as an option to consider for the end of the cosmos. At the same time, Basil demonstrated that God set the laws of creation in motion so that as the world reproduces itself, that continuous creation is under the control of God. Basil depicted God's concern, care, and providence within and to creation.

Third, Basil revealed the heart of a pastor as he developed the *Hexaemeron*. He knew that his audience needed to hear the truth of creation and that it must be reviewed in terms that are comprehended easily and not misleading. Therefore, the tone of the *Hexaemeron* is for the person who may not be developed intellectually but has the faculties to understand the truths of God's Word if presented in the proper format. He did this so the listeners' understanding was enhanced and at the same time he would not give opportunity for heretical notions to root in the mind of the listener. This approach reveals the shepherd's heart of Basil.

Finally, Basil took the concrete meaning of creation and did not scrutinize it under the guise of philosophy but took the position that philosophy must yield to the Scriptures. With that as his starting premise, he easily concluded that Genesis reveals the creation account in six literal days. The earth does not have pre-existing material, it is not old, and it did not evolve. The earth was created by God in the specified time revealed in Genesis 1 and 2 (i.e., six literal days).

Basil left Evangelicalism a wonderful gift waiting to be rediscovered for the cherished truth the *Hexaemeron* contains (i.e., God in His wisdom created the world and in His sovereignty sustains His creation until the desired eschatology is culminated).

7

BASIL SPEAKS TODAY

Basil was a man who understood his world. His ministry was related directly to the situation of Cappadocia, the church at large, and the role of the magistrates who governed fourth-century life. He could be characterized as a metropolitan pastor who spoke to ecclesiastical events beyond the boundaries of his own episcopate. As the bishop of Caesarea, his influence was extensive. Basil's role as pastor to church, community, and Christianity as a whole is a calling to guard the 'institutions and ordinances of the fathers' in order to protect and guide the Christian community into the truth of Jesus Christ.[1] Schaff, commenting about Basil, stated:

> Basil is distinguished as a pulpit orator and as a theologian, and still more as a shepherd of souls and a church ruler; and in the history of monasticism he holds a conspicuous place. In classical culture he yields to none of his contemporaries, and is justly placed with the two Gregories among the very first writers among the Greek Fathers. His style is pure, elegant, and vigorous.[2]

---

1. Fedwick, *The Church and the Charisma of Leadership in Basil*, p. 49.

2. Philip Schaff, *Nicene and Post-Nicene Christianity: From Constantine the Great to Gregory the Great A.D. 311-590*, vol. 3 of *History of the Christian Church*, p. 902.

It is no wonder that Athanasius referred to Basil as the 'true serv-ant of God'[3] who had a 'special purpose.'[4]

Ecclesiastical contributions

Basil's legacy to the Evangelical community is lasting and impres-sive. Basil, with his emphasis on holiness must become a role model who would serve to demonstrate godliness in the mod-ern world. His ability to reform monasticism reveals the heart of a man who desires that the truth of God would be lived out-wardly to a world that needs to see biblical transformation. Basil's concept of monastic community served the church in the fourth century but speaks to the heart of every theologian, pastor, staff member, and layman. The accountability of the modern leaders of the church must be regained in order to minister to a world that denies any form of accountability. Monasticism was not an easy life to pursue but neither is the calling to serve God in the church today. Yet the manner of life lived in an accountable community demonstrates the power of God at work in the ecclesia.

The sermons of Basil reveal to the Evangelical world that the Word of God is central to the Christian community. The account-ability of leadership to surrender to the authority of the Word is neglected today. Basil demonstrated that one's understanding and knowledge of the Word can grow into deeper truths. However, that knowledge is not to be contained in isolation but directed to the ministry of the ecclesia. Thus, his sermons give truth to the church for their growth in that same spiritual truth.

Two final thoughts about Basil's ecclesiastical contributions: First, he related his sermons, the liturgy, and church life at large to the theological acumen of his congregation. He did not speak below their intelligence to insult them nor did he speak above their intelligence to ridicule them. He referenced his sermons to challenge the hearts and minds of the congregants so that their spiritual growth always was foremost.

---

3. Athanasius, *Letter 62*, NPNF, vol. 4, p. 580.
4. Ibid., *Letter 63*.

Second, Basil's work in the church was not to build a personal kingdom. He revealed this as he endeavored to work at solving the problems within Christianity with other bishops and pastors. His relationship with Athanasius, Melitus, Gregory of Nyssa, Gregory of Nazianzus, and Amphilochius (to name just a few) depicts the heart of a man whose desire was to be a part of the Lord's work not only at Caesarea but throughout the world.

Today, Basil's example for Evangelicalism is that the ministry of each individual should serve the greater kingdom at large. The goal of churches serving the kingdom together is not simply a fourth-century phenomenon, but finds its foundation within the Scriptures.[5] Evangelicalism can take the biblical legacy of Basil, apply the lesson today, and work with one another for the advancement of the Lord's commission.[6] Basil's ministry still speaks today!

Theological contributions

The theological contribution of Basil is distinguished by his commitment to safeguard the church. Basil comprehended the truth that seems to be forgotten by Evangelicalism today: if the theology of the church declines, no amount of doxology can recover it. One simply cannot praise God without a firm grasp of the truth of God. Basil instinctively knew that the Holy Spirit must have His rightful place as God within the Trinity.

The work, *On the Holy Spirit*,[7] solved the Arian problem within the church. The second phase of Arianism was an ordeal that needed a cultured and theologically sophisticated leader to address the finer theological problems of the crisis. His response to Arianism via *On the Holy Spirit* remains a theological work that demands attention by the Evangelical community. Bobrinskoy aptly stated, 'The pastoral and pedagogical dimension of

---

5.   1 Corinthians 16:1–3 reveals that the churches at Galatia and Corinth were taking an offering to help the Jerusalem church in their time of need.

6.   This is a reference to the Great Commission as found in Matthew 28:18-20.

7.   See Chapter Five.

the work of St. Basil is marked by his doctrinal "economy." The significance of the proper role of the divine hypostases and of the pedagogy of the Holy Spirit remains one of the main lines of force of his theological research.'[8]

His goal for the work, On the Holy Spirit, was to establish the person of the Holy Spirit in the liturgy of the church. The idea was that the church was worshiping the Trinity (i.e., theology meets doxology in the ecclesia). Not only did the church worship the Trinitarian God but the church began to have an understanding of the different relationships within the Trinity. Thus, the fourth-century church had a solid theological foundation that expressed itself in its doxology.

The lesson for modern Evangelicalism is to recapture the truth of the Trinity so that the church can grow theologically and spiritually stronger to meet the demands of the secular critics. The worship service of the church requires a proper understanding of the God it proclaims. The secondary lesson is that even though apologetics may not be the main focus of the church, the demand to give an explanation for the faith is not only critical to the discipleship process but a biblical command.[9] The works of Basil in this area of Trinitarian studies will help the modern Evangelical world give a viable answer to the critics who advocate religious pluralism. Basil distinguished the nature of God as Trinitarian compared and contrasted to the Arian God which denied the ontological Trinity. This same lesson is available to the Evangelical world as the proclamation of God still is warranted, especially as an answer to the rival, albeit false, religions of the modern twenty-first century.

Conclusion

Basil speaks to the modern Evangelical community today as a positive lesson and as a warning. First, the warning: the Evangelical world must not forget the lesson of Basil in the face of

---

8.   Bobrinskoy, The Mystery of the Trinity, pp. 248-9.

9.   See Jude 3.

theological confrontation. He answered the critics with theological acumen that established the Word of God as supreme. The warning for today's theologian, pastor, and church is to establish the church and ministry on the foundation of the Scriptures. Without such a foundation, the house will fall.

The positive lesson is that regardless of the hardship, God calls men and women to suffer righteously for the advancement of His work. The self-denial of Basil is an example for the modern Evangelical community today. To deny oneself in order to serve others is the calling of the Master for the twenty-first century and modeled by Basil in the fourth century.

BIBLIOGRAPHY

Editions and translations

Arius. *Letter to Alexander.* Edited and translated by William G. Rusch in *The Trinitarian Controversy*, ed. and trans. William G. Rusch. *Sources of Early Christian Thought*. Philadelphia, PA: Fortress Press, 1980.

Athanasius. *Ad Afros Epistola Synodica.* Translated by Archibald Robertson in *Select Writings and Letters of Athanasius, Bishop of Alexandria*, eds. Philip Schaff and Henry Wace, *NPNF* 2nd series, vol. 4. Peabody, MA: Hendrickson Publishers, 1994.

_____. *Councils of Ariminum and Seleucia.* Translated by Archibald Robertson in *Select Writings and Letters of Athanasius, Bishop of Alexandria*, eds. Philip Schaff and Henry Wace, *NPNF* 2nd series, vol. 4. Peabody, MA: Hendrickson Publishers, 1994.

_____. *Letter 54.* Translated by Archibald Robertson in *Select Writings and Letters of Athanasius, Bishop of Alexandria*, eds. Philip Schaff and Henry Wace, *NPNF* 2nd series, vol. 4. Peabody, MA: Hendrickson Publishers, 1994.

_____. *Letter 62.* Translated by Archibald Robertson in *Select Writings and Letters of Athanasius, Bishop of Alexandria*, eds. Philip Schaff and Henry Wace, *NPNF* 2nd series, vol. 4. Peabody, MA: Hendrickson Publishers, 1994.

_____. *Letter 63.* Translated by Archibald Robertson in *Select Writings and Letters of Athanasius, Bishop of Alexandria*, eds. Philip Schaff and Henry Wace, *NPNF* 2nd series, vol. 4. Peabody, MA: Hendrickson Publishers, 1994.

_____. *The Life of Anthony*, trans. by Robert Gregg. *The Classics of Western Spirituality*. New York, NY: Paulist Press, 1980.

Augustine. *The Literal Meaning of Genesis*. Editors, Johannes Quasten, Walter J. Burghardt, Thomas Comerford Lawler, *Ancient Christian Writers*, vols. 41-2. New York, NY: Paulist Press, 1982.

Basil. *Against Eunomius*, trans. by Mark DelCogliano and Andrew Raddle-Gallwitz. Washington, D.C.: The Catholic University of America Press, 2011.

_____. *Ascetical Works*. Translated by Monica Wagner, *Fathers of the Church*, vol. 9. Washington, D.C.: Catholic University of America Press, 1950.

_____. *Hexaemeron in Exegetical Homilies*, translated by Agnes Clare Way, *Fathers of the Church*, vol. 46. Washington, D.C.: Catholic University of America Press, 1963.

_____. *Homily 13 on Psalms 28*, in *Exegetical Homilies*, translated by Agnes Clare Way, *Fathers of the Church*, vol. 46. Washington, D.C.: Catholic University of America Press, 1963.

_____. *Homily 17 on the Psalms* in *Exegetical Homilies*, translated by Agnes Clare Way, *Fathers of the Church*, vol. 46. Washington, D.C.: Catholic University of America Press, 1963.

_____. *I Will Tear Down My Barns*. Translated by C. Paul Schroeder in *On Social Justice*. Crestwood, NY: St. Vladimir's Seminary Press, 2009.

_____. *Letter 2*, trans. by Roy J. Deferrari, 4 vols. New York, NY: G. P. Putnam's Sons, 1926.

_____. *Letter 9*. Translated by Blomfield Jackson in *Basil: Letters and Select Works*, eds. Philip Schaff and Henry Wace, *NPNF* 2nd series, vol. 8. Peabody, MA: Hendrickson Publishers, 1994.

_____. *Letter 34*. Translated by Blomfield Jackson. In *Basil: Letters and Select Works*. eds. Philip Schaff and Henry Wace, *NPNF* 2nd series, vol. 8. Peabody, MA: Hendrickson Publishers, 1994.

_____. *Letter 66*. Translated by Blomfield Jackson in *Basil: Letters and Select Works*, eds. Philip Schaff and Henry Wace, *NPNF* 2nd series, vol. 8. Peabody, MA: Hendrickson Publishers, 1994.

_____. *Letter 67.* Translated by Blomfield Jackson in *Basil: Letters and Select Works*, eds. Philip Schaff and Henry Wace, *NPNF* 2nd series, vol. 8. Peabody, MA: Hendrickson Publishers, 1994.

_____. *Letter 69.* Translated by Blomfield Jackson in *Basil: Letters and Select Works*, eds. Philip Schaff and Henry Wace, *NPNF* 2nd series, vol. 8. Peabody, MA: Hendrickson Publishers, 1994.

_____. *Letter 74.* Translated by Blomfield Jackson in *Basil: Letters and Select Works*, eds. Philip Schaff and Henry Wace, *NPNF* 2nd series, vol. 8. Peabody, MA: Hendrickson Publishers, 1994.

_____. *Letter 82.* Translated by Blomfield Jackson in *Basil: Letters and Select Works*, eds. Philip Schaff and Henry Wace, *NPNF* 2nd series, vol. 8. Peabody, MA: Hendrickson Publishers, 1994.

_____. *Letter 89,* trans. by Roy J. Deferrari, 4 vols. New York, NY: G. P. Putnam's Sons, 1926.

_____. *Letter 99.* Translated by Blomfield Jackson in *Basil: Letters and Select Works*. eds. Philip Schaff and Henry Wace, *NPNF* 2nd series, vol. 8. Peabody, MA: Hendrickson Publishers, 1994.

_____. *Letter 113.* Translated by Blomfield Jackson in *Basil: Letters and Select Works*, eds. Philip Schaff and Henry Wace, *NPNF* 2nd series, vol. 8. Peabody, MA: Hendrickson Publishers, 1994.

_____. *Letter 125.* Translated by Blomfield Jackson in *Basil: Letters and Select Works*, eds. Philip Schaff and Henry Wace, *NPNF* 2nd series, vol. 8. Peabody, MA: Hendrickson Publishers, 1994.

_____. *Letter 161.* Translated by Blomfield Jackson in *Basil: Letters, and Select Works*, eds. Philip Schaff and Henry Wace, *NPNF* 2nd series, vol. 8. Peabody, MA: Hendrickson Publishers, 1994.

_____. *Letter 214.* Translated by Blomfield Jackson in *Basil: Letters and Select Works*, eds. Philip Schaff and Henry Wace, *NPNF* 2nd series, vol. 8. Peabody, MA: Hendrickson Publishers, 1994.

_____. *Letter 215.* Translated by Blomfield Jackson in *Basil: Letters and Select Works*, eds. Philip Schaff and Henry Wace, *NPNF* 2nd series, vol. 8. Peabody, MA: Hendrickson Publishers, 1994.

————. *Letter 223.* Translated by Blomfield Jackson in *Basil: Letters and Select Works*, eds. Philip Schaff and Henry Wace, *NPNF* 2nd series, vol. 8. Peabody, MA: Hendrickson Publishers, 1994.

————. *Letter 244.* Translated by Blomfield Jackson in *Basil: Letters and Select Works*, eds. Philip Schaff and Henry Wace, *NPNF* 2nd series, vol. 8. Peabody, MA: Hendrickson Publishers, 1994.

————. *On the Holy Spirit*, trans. by David Anderson. Crestwood, NY: St. Vladimir's Seminary Press, 1980.

Eusebius. *Letter to Paulinus, Bishop of Tyre.* Translated by Blomfield Jackson in *The Ecclesiastical History, Dialogues, and Letters of Theodoret*, eds. Philip Schaff and Henry Wace, *NPNF*, 2nd series, vol. 3. Peabody, MA: Hendrickson Publishers, 1994.

Gregory of Nazianzen. *Letter to Gregory of Nyssa.* Translated by Charles Gordon Browne and James Edward Swallow in *Saint Gregory of Nazianzen*, American ed. *NPNF* 2nd series, vol. 7. Peabody, MA: Hendrickson Publishers, 2006.

————. *The Panegyric on St. Basil.* Translated by Charles Gordon Browne and James Edward Swallow in *Saint Gregory of Nazianzen*, eds. Philip Schaff and Henry Wace, *NPNF* 2nd series, vol. 7. Peabody, MA: Hendrickson Publishers, 2006.

Gregory of Nyssa. *Letter to Adelphius.* Translated by William Moore and Henry Austin Wilson in *Gregory of Nyssa*, eds. Philip Schaff and Henry Wace, *NPNF* 2nd series, vol. 5. Peabody, MA: Hendrickson Publishers, 2006.

————. *Letter to Libanius.* Translated by William Moore and Henry Austin Wilson in *Gregory of Nyssa*, eds. Philip Schaff and Henry Wace, *NPNF* 2nd series, vol. 5. Peabody, MA: Hendrickson Publishers, 2006.

————. *Life of Macrina*, trans. by W. K. Lowther Clarke. London: Society for Promoting Christian Knowledge, 1916.

Jerome. *The Dialogue against the Luciferians.* Translated by Ernest Cushing Richardson in *Theodoret, Jerome, Gennadius, Rufinus, Historical Writings*, eds. Philip Schaff and Henry Wace, *NPNF* 2nd series, vol. 3. Peabody, MA: Hendrickson Publishers, 2006.

Socrates Scholasticus. *Church History: From A.D. 305–439.* Translated by A.C. Zenos in *Socrates, Sozomenus, Church Histories*, eds. Philip Schaff and Henry Wace, *NPNF* 2nd series, vol. 2. Peabody, MA: Hendrickson Publishers, 2006.

Sozomenus. *History of the Church.* Translated by Chester D. Hartranft in *Socrates, Sozomenus, Church Histories*, eds. Philip Schaff and Henry Wace, *NPNF* 2nd series, vol. 2. Peabody, MA: Hendrickson Publishers, 2006.

Theodoret. *The Ecclesiastical History.* Translated by Blomfield Jackson in *The Ecclesiastical History, Dialogues, and Letters of Theodoret*, eds. Philip Schaff and Henry Wace, *NPNF*, 2nd series, vol. 3. Peabody, MA: Hendrickson Publishers, 1994.

Books and Journal Articles

Behr, John. *The Nicene Faith.* Crestwood, NY: St. Vladimir's Seminary Press, 2004.

Berkhof, Louis. *The History of Christian Doctrines.* Grand Rapids, MI: Baker Book House Publishing Co., 1996.

Bobrinskoy, Boris. 'The Indwelling of the Spirit of Christ: "Pneumatic Christology" in the Cappadocian Fathers.' *St. Vladimir's Theological Quarterly* 28:1 (January 1, 1984): 49–65.

_____. *The Mystery of the Trinity: Trinitarian Experience and Vision in the Biblical and Patristic Tradition.* Crestwood, NY: St. Vladimir's Seminary Press, 1999.

Brown, Harold O. J. *Heresies.* Garden City, NY: Doubleday & Co., 1984.

Callahan, John F. 'Basil of Caesarea: A New Source for St. Augustine's Theory of Time.' *Harvard Studies in Classical Philology* 63 (1958): 437–54.

Chadwick, Henry. *The Early Church.* London, England: Penguin Books, 1993.

Clarke, William Kemp Lowther. *Saint Basil the Great: A Study in Monasticism.* Cambridge: Cambridge University Press, 1912.

Constantelos, Demetrios J. 'Basil the Great's Social Thought and Involvement.' *The Greek Orthodox Theological Review* 2:1-2 (March 1, 1981): 81–6.

Davies, Michael. *Saint Athanasius: Defender of the Faith*. Kansas City, MO: Angelus Press, 2001.

DelCogliano, Mark. 'Basil of Caesarea's Anti-Eunomian Theory of Names.' Ph.D. diss., Emory University, 2009.

_____. *Introduction to the Work against Eunomius*. Washington: The Catholic University of America Press, 2011.

Dockery, David. *Christian Perspective: An Evangelical Perspective on Inspiration, Authority and Interpretation*. Nashville, TN: Broadman and Holman Publishers, 1995.

Dragas, George Dion. *Saint Athanasius of Alexandria: Original Research and New Perspectives*. Rollinsford, NH: Orthodox Research Institute, 2005.

Drobner, Hubertus R. *The Fathers of the Church: A Comprehensive Introduction*, trans. Siegfried S. Schatzmann. Peabody, MA: Hendrickson Publishers, 2007.

Durant, William. *The Age of Faith*. Vol. IV of *The Story of Civilization*. New York, NY: Simon and Schuster, 1950.

Fedwick, Paul Jonathan. *The Church and the Charisma of Leadership in Basil of Caesarea*. Toronto: Pontifical Institute of Medieval Studies, 1979.

Florovsky, Georges. 'The Function of Tradition in the Ancient Church.' *The Greek Orthodox Theological Review* 9:2 (1963): 73-92.

Frazee, Charles A. 'Anatolian Asceticism in the Fourth Century: Eustathios of Sebastea and Basil of Caesarea.' *The Catholic Historical Review* 66:1 (Jan. 1980): 16-33.

Giet, S. *Basile de Césarée, Homélies sur L'Hexaméron*. Paris, 1950.

Gribomont, Jean. 'Intransigence and Irenicism in Saint Basil's "De Spiritu Sancto".' In *Honor of Saint Basil the Great*. Still River, MA: St. Bede's Publications, 1979.

Griffith, Howard. 'The Churchly Theology of Basil's *De Spiritu Sancto*.' *Presbyterion* 25:2 (1999): 91-108.

Harmless, William. *Desert Christians: An Introduction to the Literature of Early Monasticism*. Oxford, England: Oxford University Press, 2004.

Haykin, Michael A. G. *A Fence around a Mystery: The Niceno-Constantino-politan Creed, Its Background and Teaching,* 10. This article was forwarded by the author. No publication data is available for a complete bibliographical entry.

_____. 'Defending the Holy Spirit's Deity: Basil of Caesarea, Gregory of Nyssa, and the Pneumatomachian Controversy of the 4th Century.' *Southern Baptist Journal of Theology* 73 (Fall 2003):74-9.

_____. *Rediscovering the Church Fathers.* Wheaton, IL: Crossway, 2011.

_____. *The Spirit of God: The Exegesis of 1 & 2 Corinthians in the Pneumatomachian Controversy of the Fourth Century.* Leiden, Netherlands: E. J. Brill, 1994.

Hildebrand, Stephen M. *The Trinitarian Theology of Basil of Caesarea.* Washington, D.C.: The Catholic University of America Press, 2007.

Holmes, Augustine. *The Spirituality of the Rules of St. Basil.* Kalamazoo, MI: Cistercian Publications, 2000.

Kelly, J. N. D. *Early Christian Doctrines.* San Francisco, CA: Harper Collins Publishing, 1978.

Kerr, Hugh Thomson. *Preaching in the Early Church.* New York, NY: Fleming H. Revell Company, 1942.

Khodr, Metropolitan Georges. 'Basil the Great: Bishop and Pastor.' *St. Vladimir's Theological Quarterly* 29 (Jan. 1985): 5-27.

Letham, Robert. *The Holy Trinity: In Scripture, History, Theology, and Worship.* Phillipsburg, NJ: P&R Publishing, 2004.

Lienhard, Joseph T. 'Basil of Caesarea, Marcellus of Ancyra, and Sabellius.' *Church History* 58:2 (June 1989): 157-67.

_____. *Contra Marcellum: Marcellus of Ancyra and Fourth-Century Theology.* Washington, D.C.: The Catholic University of America Press, 1999.

Lim, Richard. 'The Politics of Interpretation in Basil of Caesarea's Hexaemeron.' *Vigiliae Christianae* 44 (1990): 351-70.

Molloy, Michael E. *Champion of Truth: The Life of Saint Athanasius.* New York, NY: Alba House, 2003.

Murphy, Margaret. *St. Basil and Monasticism.* New York, NY: AMS Press, 1971.

Osborn, Ronald E. 'I'm Looking Over a Four-leaf Clover that I Overlooked ...The Cappadocians Reconsidered.' *Impact* 8 (1982): 15–30.

Pelikan, Jaroslav. 'The "Spiritual Sense" of Scripture; The Exegetical Basis for St. Basil's Doctrine of the Holy Spirit.' *Basil of Caesarea: Christian, Humanist, Ascetic: A Sixteenth-Hundred Anniversary Symposium,* ed. Paul J. Fedwick. Toronto: Pontifical Institute of Medieval Studies, 1981.

Prestige, G. L. *St. Basil the Great and Apollinaris of Laodicea.* London: S.P.C.K., 1956.

Rahner, Karl. *The Trinity.* New York, NY: Crossroad Publishing, 1997.

Reilly, Gerald R. *Imperium and Sacerdotium According to St. Basil the Great.* Washington, DC: The Catholic University of America Press, 1945.

Rousseau, Philip. *Basil of Caesarea.* Los Angeles, CA: University of California Press, 1994.

Rusch, William G. *The Trinitarian Controversy.* Philadelphia, PA: Fortress Press, 1980.

Schaff, Philip. *Nicene and Post-Nicene Christianity: From Constantine the Great to Gregory the Great A.D. 311–590,* vol. 3 of *History of the Christian Church.* Peabody, MA: Hendricksen Publishers, 2006.

Schroeder, C. Paul. *Introduction to On Social Justice.* Crestwood, NY: St. Vladimir's Seminary Press, 2009.

Shelley, Bruce. *Church History in Plain Language.* Dallas, TX: Word Publishing, 1982.

Siecienski, Edward. *The Filioque: History of a Doctrinal Controversy.* Oxford: Oxford University Press, 2010.

Turcescu, Lucian. 'Prosopon and Hypostasis in Basil of Caesarea's "Against Eunomius" and the Epistles.' *Vigiliae Christianae* 51:4 (1997): 374–95.

Vaggione, R. P. *Eunomius: The Extant Works,* ed. by R. P. Vaggione, Oxford Early Christian Texts. Oxford: Clarendon Press, 1987.

Vogüé, Adalbert de. 'The Greater Rules of Saint Basil – A Survey.' *Word and Spirit, A Monastic Review*, ed. S.M. Clare. Still River, MA: St. Bede's Publications, 1979.

Walker, Williston. *A History of the Christian Church*. New York, NY: Charles Scribner's Sons Publishing, 1985.

Wilken, Robert L. 'The Spirit of Holiness: Basil of Caesarea and Early Christian Spirituality.' *Worship* 42:2 (Fall 1968): 77–87.

Winden, J. C. M Van. 'In the Beginning: Some Observations of the Patristic Interpretation of *Genesis 1:1*.' *Vigiliae Christianae* 17 (1963): 105–121.

Young, Frances. *From Nicaea to Chalcedon*. Philadelphia, PA: Fortress Press, 1983

Christian Focus Publications

Our mission statement –

STAYING FAITHFUL
In dependence upon God we seek to impact the world through literature faithful to His infallible Word, the Bible. Our aim is to ensure that the Lord Jesus Christ is presented as the only hope to obtain forgiveness of sin, live a useful life and look forward to heaven with Him.

Our Books are published in four imprints:

CHRISTIAN
FOCUS

popular works including biographies, commentaries, basic doctrine and Christian living.

CHRISTIAN
HERITAGE

books representing some of the best material from the rich heritage of the church.

MENTOR

books written at a level suitable for Bible College and seminary students, pastors, and other serious readers. The imprint includes commentaries, doctrinal studies, examination of current issues and church history.

CF4•K

children's books for quality Bible teaching and for all age groups: Sunday school curriculum, puzzle and activity books; personal and family devotional titles, biographies and inspirational stories – Because you are never too young to know Jesus!

Christian Focus Publications Ltd,
Geanies House, Fearn, Ross-shire,
IV20 1TW, Scotland, United Kingdom.
www.christianfocus.com